# The Gods Within

# The Gods Within

## The Pagan Pathfinders Book of God and Goddess Evocations

### Jean M. Williams and Zachary Cox

Moondust Books

Published in Great Britain in 2008 by

Moondust Books Ltd
PO Box 36786, London, SW9 9YX, UK
www.moondustbooks.biz

British Library Cataloguing in Publication Data.
A catalogue record for this book is available
from the British Library

ISBN 978-0-9547498-1-1

Front cover photo and Pagan Pathfinders Tree by Sue Ritchie
Back cover photo by Ruth Bayer

Printed and bound in Great Britain
Biddles Ltd, King's Lynn, Norfolk

# Contents

About the Authors                                    7

## *Introduction*
The Power of Myth                                   16
Pagan Pathfinders                                   17
Archetypes                                          18
Why "Evocations"?                                   19
"God-casting"                                       21
The Format of the Evocations                        24
Why these Goddesses and Gods?                       25
Responsible Use of these Evocations                 26

Acknowledgements                                    30

## *Goddesses & Gods*

### *Graeco-Roman*
Aphrodite                                           32
Apollo                                              41
Ares                                                48
Artemis                                             56

Athene                64
Dionysus              74
Hermes                82
Magna Mater           92
Pan                  103
Persephone           110
Zeus                 118

*Egyptian*
Bast                 126
Nut                  136
Sekhmet              144

*Celtic*
The Morrigan         154

Bibliography         160

# *About the Authors*

*Z*achary Cox and Jean M. Williams have been partners in magical and esoteric activities since 1965, each bringing their own complementary talents to what has been a very fruitful partnership.

**Zach** was born in 1930 in a Victorian Gothic house in Folkestone cemetery where his father was the superintendent. His playground was a vast green acreage of trees, tombstones and family vaults, an ideal place for an imaginative and energetic child. His mother used to read him Edgar Alan Poe by candlelight and both parents passed on to him a love of words and the music of words in prose, poetry and song. In his early teens he became interested in science fiction and fantasy, and in magical and philosophical ideas. The work of Eliphas Levi introduced him to the Kabbalah and a new symbolic vocabulary. A poster advertising lectures at the Folkestone Theosophical Society caught his eye because around the poster was depicted one of these Kabbalistic symbols: a serpent with its tail in its mouth and the words, "There is no religion higher than Truth". He decided to explore further and visited the local headquarters where he met some interesting, if rather elderly, people who seemed eager to encourage the interest of youngsters. He discovered that they had an extensive library of which he took full advantage, exploring not only Theosophy but comparative religion, magic and philosophy.

National Service at the age of eighteen took Zach to London where he contacted the Youth Branch of the Theosophical Society. There he met his friend and mentor, John Gordon. John was several years older than Zach; he had served as a major in the Indian army and was posted to Egypt during the war. He had a deep and extensive knowledge of mysticism and occult philosophy through which he conveyed his own unique wisdom. They remained friends for fifty years, until John's death.

After National Service, Zach returned to Folkestone, married and set about the task of earning a living and bringing up a family, writing poetry when the inspiration took him and getting a few short stories published in various magazines and journals. He maintained his interest in magic and his friendship with John Gordon. A lurid expose of Gerald Gardner's coven in the *Sunday People* prompted him to write to the newspaper and complain. To their credit, they passed his letter on to the coven, which contacted Zach and invited him to go to Brickett Wood, a nudist club near St. Albans where the coven met; there he met Gerald Gardner. Although elderly and not in good health, Gardner was still full of life and mischief.

Zach's new contacts opened doors to a new career as a computer programmer and his world changed. He had a natural affinity for programming and advanced rapidly. He then moved to London, where both he and his wife found new loves and separated their domestic lives. Zach went to live with Jean in Hampstead and then, in 1968, they purchased the house in Crouch End where they still live.

**Jean's** background was, in contrast, more conventional. The third child of a Church of England clergyman, her father died in 1932 when she was only four years old and her mother had to return to her interrupted career as a teacher. The education of the three children was financed by a philanthropic C. of E. society and they became boarders at minor public schools with chapel twice a day. The education Jean received was academically good (if intellectual curiosity and emotional development were neglected) and Jean went on to obtain a degree in Psychology at University College, London. This was in the late 1940s when the majority of university students were recently demobbed ex-service men and women, considerably more sophisticated than the naïve girl from a C. of E. boarding school. Going home on the Tube one day, Jean was mulling over the disparate ideas with which she was being bombarded within the context of her hitherto unquestioning acceptance of Christianity as *the* revealed religion.

Suddenly, the thought occurred, "Perhaps it's not true!" And it felt as though a great weight fell from her shoulders. There followed ten years of happy agnosticism during which she established herself as a research psychologist working in the area of survey research.

The 1960s brought the psychedelic revolution, flower power, the Beatles and exciting new ideas about mental health and self-fulfilment. Personal growth was no longer considered to stop on reaching adulthood but instead was held to be a life-long process of discovery, development and self-realisation. The works of Abraham Maslow, R. D. Laing, Eric Berne, Charles Rycroft, Wilhelm Reich and many others were turning psychotherapy on its head. There was a resurgence of interest in the writings of the Swiss psychoanalyst Carl Jung; his theories of archetypes and the collective unconscious were seen as bringing coherence to such phenomena as extra-sensory perception and the sense of the continuity and interflow of all things that was experienced by users of psychedelics.

Psychedelics, such as mescalin and LSD and to a lesser extent cannabis, were seen as opening "The Doors of Perception", leading to spiritual experience and insight. Aldous Huxley's book of that title in which he describes his own mescalin experience, fired Jean's imagination. There was also at that time an influx of eastern philosophical ideas and practices. Jean began to feel that something was missing from her life, something much larger than the anodyne Christianity of her school days.

She met Zach and other members of the coven in 1961; they seemed to be on a similar quest for a spiritual dimension. A shared mescalin experiment, carefully orchestrated by an experienced researcher in psychedelics (mescalin was still legal at that time), was a very profound experience that led to a deep interest in Zen Buddhism, inner exploration, meditation and a yearning for self-fulfilment. At that time the Gardnerian Craft of Wicca was strictly esoteric, but Alex Sanders was publicizing his own version of it and by the late 60s an exoteric Paganism was starting to develop, assisted by a number of small Pagan magazines through which ideas were shared.

**Jean and Zach together:** The early 1970s were testing times with Zach having a serious bout of manic-depressive illness and Jean intensively exploring the Human Potential Movement and the new humanistic therapies.

Jean had tried one-to-one therapy with a psychoanalyst in the mid-60s but had got very little out of it. Humanistic psychology, on the other hand, offered a whole range of new approaches for those who managed their lives adequately but had this urge to reach ever forward in personal growth and self-realisation. Rather than a patient-therapist relationship, there was client and facilitator; much of the work was done in groups rather than individually and each participant was responsible for themselves, trusted to open themselves only as much as they felt comfortable with, to share or to remain quiet, to support others or to hold back. But what was expected was honesty, compassion and a willingness to understand others' points of view. The techniques are enormously variable, including encounter, body work to release the tensions that hold emotional baggage in place, dream analysis, psychodrama, drawing, use of the active imagination, role-playing and role-swapping, and many more. Group meetings were often extremely noisy, with participants releasing the pent-up anger of years, but ended with feelings of love, euphoria and high energy. What was noticeable was that when people had done a lot of work freeing themselves up, they often tended to start to feel the need for a spiritual dimension to their lives. Wanting something other than the orthodox western religions, they turned to the East – notably to the Maharishi Mahesh Yogi, guru to the Beatles and founder of Transcendental Meditation, or to Bhagwan Shree Rajneesh and his Dynamic Meditation.

At the same time, the Pagan scene was continuing to develop: conferences, magazines and books on witchcraft, magical practices and mythology were proliferating; Pagans of various denominations were becoming more public and their numbers were increasing rapidly. But there seemed to be little interchange between this and the Human Potential Movement: Pagan groups were notorious for splitting up acrimoniously, having no tools with which to handle disagreement and anger; and Human Potential people continued to turn to the east for spiritual sustenance, being largely unaware of their own indigenous western spiritual paths. Awareness of this gap between two important developments led Jean to organise two "Bridges and Boundaries" conferences with a mixture of talks and humanistic workshops, but these involved a great deal of work and another approach was sought. The concept of a smaller weekly evening group took hold and in 1975, with Zach's active help, Pagan Pathfinders was born.

Pagan Pathfinders, for which the evocations in this book were written, was designed to be a synthesis of Pagan spiritual practices and humanistic psychology. It ushered in the most active and creative period of Jean and Zach's collaboration. 1975 was also the 100th anniversary of Aleister Crowley's birth which Jean and Zach celebrated with a performance of his Gnostic Mass. This magnificent ritual had such a profound effect that they decided to continue to perform it twice a year.

In 1977, they founded the Companions of the Rainbow Bridge, a ritual drama group designed to provide training in the development of the ritual persona and the writing, production and performance of ritual. The Companions took over the organisation of the Gnostic Mass and performances were increased to four times a year, each time with a congregation of personally invited guests. With a couple of periods of quiescence, the Rainbow Bridge kept going until the mid-nineties, leaving a legacy of over forty rituals, many of them brilliant original works. 1977 also saw the start of Zach's magazine *Aquarian Arrow*, a publication that was libertarian, provocative, controversial, philosophical, satirical and profound. It ran for 34 issues over a period of about fifteen years.

In the 1990s, first Jean, then Zach, became involved in the running of the Pagan Federation, an organization founded in 1971 to protect Pagans and Paganism from the defamation and harassment that was common at that time, especially in the tabloids. Jean assumed the *nom de guerre* of "Elen Williams" within the Pagan Federation, partly to distinguish herself from another Jean Williams who wrote a book called *Winning with Witchcraft*, but primarily to protect herself from exposure by the tabloids: she became PF President at the height of the ritual child abuse scare in the early 90s and was in the vanguard of the fight to protect Pagans from defamation and false accusations. At the time of writing Jean and Zach still maintain the PF database and serve on the Council as Honorary Members.

Having told our story dispassionately and now both in our seventies, we look back on the 1970s and 80s, when we were both working in full-time professional careers, and wonder how we ever managed to do so much! This book is what we hope will be the first of our attempts to harvest the fruits of those years and to share them with a wider public.

Jean wrote the essays in this book; Zach wrote the majority of the Evocations.

Jean and Zach
2008

# *Introduction*

**The Power of Myth**

The goddesses and gods of ancient civilisations have an evocative power that intrigues and fascinates modern Pagans. Their myths originated long ago in societies very different from our own, yet the stories encapsulate truths about forces that still affect us. When we penetrate beneath the surface of myths, we discover resonances with personal, spiritual and social issues that have their parallels today and that all of us have to deal with in our lives. Our mythic heritage is huge and extraordinarily rich. The essays and evocations in this book are based on just a few of the more familiar myths from ancient Greece, Rome, Egypt and our Celtic heritage. The essays summarise the characteristics and qualities of each god-form as presented in myth and describe their relevance to our lives today. The evocations are designed to draw forth the inner essence of the mythological gods and goddesses and to make the qualities of the forces they represent accessible and empowering.

The precursor to this volume was a small booklet consisting of eleven evocations (without essays) of goddesses and gods mainly from the Graeco-Roman pantheons; it was published by the Neopantheist Society in 1979. The evocations were developed for use in the Pagan Pathfinders group workshops.

## Pagan Pathfinders

Pagan Pathfinders is a weekly experiential group, working with a combination of Pagan mythic elements, traditional spiritual disciplines and the modern techniques of humanistic psychology. Its purpose is to facilitate inner exploration, personal growth and empowerment, providing participants with tools that they can use in their everyday lives. The methods and images employed are designed to expand our consciousness, to heighten our awareness of the natural world, of life and death and renewal, and of the great cycles of Nature, of the sun, moon and stars; and also to look within, to find there the reflections and harmonics of the cosmic forces, the interplay of which shape our lives. It encompasses the basics of meditation, deep relaxation, energy-raising, the use of active imagination and inner creativity. The techniques used are varied; they include dance, quiet reflection, visualisation, creative writing, drawing, informal ritual, chanting and music making. It follows no specific Pagan path or pantheon and uses both eastern and western techniques, ritual forms and mythologies.

## Archetypes

Goddesses and gods from different pantheons are explored in Pagan Pathfinders and in these essays. Within this context, the god-forms are regarded as representations of archetypal forces, not as "spirits of place" or discrete entities. The concept of archetypes was introduced by the psychologist Carl Jung following his comparative study of myths and god-forms from around the world. He saw similar patterns emerging within the mythic systems of many different cultures and identified them as representing universal forces that are seen within the individual psyche, within society and within the natural world – cosmic forces that work within us, through us and around us. In Pagan Pathfinders and through these evocations we seek to contact these archetypal forces in order to access our sources of inner wisdom and to enhance particular inner qualities.

The Pagan goddesses and gods are not images of idealised perfection. They are fundamental forces within Nature and within the human psyche. The myths tell of their loves and hates, of their jealousies and vengefulness, of their conflicts and abuses of power, as well as of their beneficence, generosity, and nurturing and inspirational qualities: Aphrodite, Goddess of Love and Beauty, becomes unreasonably jealous when her son, Cupid, falls in love with Psyche; Zeus, the King of the

Olympian gods, constantly flouts his own rules about social order by letting his lusty exuberance lead him into a series of sexual encounters with nymphs and human women, begetting a large number of demi-gods. The goddesses and gods are archetypal expressions of human vices and virtues, strengths and weaknesses, writ large. But their powers are in themselves innocent; neither good nor bad: their "vices" are strengths taken to excess, unbalanced by other qualities; their "weaknesses" are due to the lack of counterbalancing virtues. Each pantheon of Pagan goddesses and gods contains within it a rich variety of archetypal beings who between them represent the full range of human psychological qualities, constituting a balanced whole. Evocation provides a valuable tool that we can utilise to enhance our own inner balance. By evoking within ourselves the qualities of a particular goddess or god, we can strengthen those attributes in which we are weak and counterbalance aspects of our natures that we find hard to control.

## Why "Evocations"?

Why do we call these offerings *"evocations"* rather than *"invocations"*? The two terms are often used as though they were interchangeable, but it is worth making a distinction between them. Traditionally, the occult use of the word *"evocation"* has referred to the magical practice of summoning a spirit or demon into manifestation in a triangle set outside a magic circle and to establish command over it, commonly regarded as a rather dangerous operation. This is not what we do in Pagan Pathfinders nor is it the purpose of these evocations. The term is used in a psychological rather than a magical sense; the aim is to evoke feelings, images and ideas from within the psyche of the individual. The goddesses and gods represent the archetypal forces within the universe as perceived from Planet Earth and clothed in symbolic form by the human mind. These forces permeate Nature and, since we are part of Nature, they are both within us and without. Each of these evocations is designed to find the harmonics of a particular archetypal force within ourselves and to amplify it so that we experience its power and qualities as part of ourselves. Through this process, we are able to enhance particular aspects of our inner nature and to manifest them more strongly or in a more balanced way in our lives. The object is to bring about inner change, growth and empowerment.

An *invocation*, on the other hand, usually takes place within a ritual context and the object is to contact the force "out there" in the cosmos and, through an intensity of intent, to draw it down as a palpable presence, perhaps into the person of a priestess or priest. This may be for a magical or celebratory purpose. The god-force may be communed with to seek guidance and wisdom; it may be asked to grant a blessing or perhaps to bring healing or some other benefit; or this force might be directed so as to achieve some magical objective. When the force is dismissed, it may leave the personality unchanged (though not necessarily so, since a powerful experience of a god or goddess archetypal force is bound to have an effect).

It is easy to blur the distinction between evocation and invocation but it is one that it is worth maintaining. However, with minor changes the evocations in this book can be (and have been) used as invocations. The main difference is one of context and intent.

## "God-casting"

The original eleven evocations were designed for use in a technique called "god-casting", developed in the early years of Pagan Pathfinders when the group was quite small; it is a little cumbersome for use with more than five or six participants. "God-casting" consists of assigning a particular Pagan goddess or god to each member of the group, and then evoking the qualities and powers of that particular divinity within the person. The Group Leader has everyone seated with eyes closed and prepares them with relaxation exercises, meditation and guided visualisation. The

Leader then goes to each member in turn, burns an appropriate incense, and reads aloud the evocation, with maximum intention to communicate with and call forth that aspect of the person's higher nature which corresponds to the divinity concerned.

When all the goddesses and gods have been evoked, a guided meditation ensues wherein all the "gods" meet and greet each other, and then repair to their individual temples where each is enthroned and experiences their god-head. Each then sees their human manifestation entering the temple as a humble worshipper and supplicant, seeking the aid of the deity. The person thus deals with her- or him-self from a position of divine altitude, imparting wisdom, broadening horizons, revealing opportunities but, above all, experiencing the power and qualities of that god-force so that their sense of self is expanded and enhanced.

Obviously, in a group, there is a perennial problem of pre-assignment of goddesses and gods: it is not desirable to have two Hermes or three Aphrodites in the same session because this would reduce the reality and dilute the sense of identification. Apart from this constraint, the pre-assignment of divinities is in any case something of an art in itself: the deity is selected to balance up the current personality rather than merely to reflect it. On one occasion, a visiting

American lady, who in her human person was practically an incarnation of Artemis, and who was therefore convinced she would be so cast, was shattered to find herself cast as Persephone; the Group Leader had judged this to be the optimum wavelength required to balance the personality at that time. There are limits though – it would have been counter-productive to evoke the Magna Mater, for instance, because it was too far away from her current life situation and reality.

The evocations have also been used one at a time in a group context: for example, the evocation of Ares was read and the entire group then identified with this archetypal image, taking up physical postures to express it, all against a suitable musical background – in this case "Mars" from Holst's *Planets* suite. They can be used in similar ways in individual meditation to enhance an aspect of one's personality or to empower one to tackle some particular problem or endeavour.

These archetypes are universal and there is no reason why god qualities should not be evoked in women or goddess qualities in men. There is much room for exploration and experimentation in rejecting the gender stereotypes of our culture which tend to assume that, whereas women are empowered by developing what are perceived as masculine traits, men are disempowered by developing what are perceived as feminine traits.

Sections of these evocations have also been transplanted into formal rituals and used as invocations. The declamatory style of the evocations makes them eminently suitable for ceremonial use.

## The Format of the Evocations

The evocations have a standard overall format, each consisting of four sections. The first is a descriptive address to build up the magical image while establishing an "I – Thou" stance toward the divinity. The second amounts to an injunction to the divinity to "Do Its Thing"; it is an evocation of the power of that archetypal force, aligning the Will of the evocator with that of the deity, but in an active and imperative mode. The third section relates the divinity's manifestation to the life of creatures on this planet and in this plane, to earth the force into real human experience. The fourth section is the evocation proper, a series of mythically and dramatically cogent imprecations building in every case to the climax:

> "I call upon thee to be with us
> in body and in spirit!"

## Why these Goddesses and Gods?

The preponderance of Graeco-Roman goddesses and gods in these evocations is deliberate: their myths are woven deeply into Western European culture; the remains of their temples are widely scattered throughout the Mediterranean region and as far afield as Britain. Under their Roman names they people our skies, rotating in an intricate dance against the backdrop of the stars. Above all, they play a vital role in astrological lore. It is through the study of astrology that many have developed their knowledge of the qualities and characteristics of the planetary archetypes; and a study of one's own astrological chart may give pointers as to which of these evocations it might be appropriate to use.

The choice of which goddesses and gods to include was inevitably a personal one. In this volume, Pan has been added to the original ten from the Greek pantheon. The great felines, Sekhmet and Bast, join Nut, previously the only representative of the Egyptian pantheon – a mythology so rich that it warrants a book of its own. The Celtic gods are becoming increasingly popular among many modern Pagans as they seek to connect to the mythic roots of the British Isles; however, only one, the Morrigan, is included here since she covers a particular archetypal aspect not well represented elsewhere.

## Responsible use of these Evocations

These evocations were developed for use in a group situation with a leader overseeing the proceedings and providing an opportunity for discussion and evaluation afterwards. If the evocations are used in personal work, it is recommended that they are performed within a simple ritual framework: for example, visualise a protective circle of light around yourself, take a few moments to relax, emptying and focusing the mind; then in your imagination create an appropriate place around you. This might be a temple, a hillside, the starry night sky – whatever image presents itself to you from the essay or the evocation as befitting the goddess or god you wish to experience. Then read the evocation, silently or aloud, slowly, letting the ideas and images build up the sense of the inner presence of the deity, feeling yourself aligning your energies with those of the deity. Another approach might be to record the evocation first so that you can simply listen to it. Then have a period of silent meditation and inner exploration, perhaps, as in the original Pagan Pathfinders method, visualise yourself as the deity throned in your temple, and see your everyday self coming to worship and hear your wisdom.

You might choose to burn incense or perfumed oil to heighten the effect and create an appropriate atmosphere. Suggested incenses are given for each evocation. Some of these are based on long association with a particular deity but choice of incense is essentially a matter of intuition and personal taste.

If you choose to use the evocations with a partner or in a group situation, or to use them as invocations rather than evocations, discuss fully what you are trying to do and why – and trust your intuition.

Unlike the monotheisms, modern polytheist and pantheist Paganism does not lay down a set of moral rules by which humans should live. It is held that each individual is responsible for finding within themselves the wellsprings of their own ethical nature. Humans are social creatures and there is a constant inner dialectic between the desire for individual freedom and the desire to build a good society and to play a significant and constructive role within it. The spiritual and psychological growth of the individual is inextricably bound up with the quality of the interactions they have with others. In the search for wholeness and fulfilment, there is a constant need for ethical and moral evaluation and choice.

How the evocatory tools presented here are used is the responsibility of the individual using them, a responsibility that extends to the effects on others. The objective is to empower through *balance*. Overuse of a particular god-form can increase imbalance, particularly with some of the more aggressive and uncompromising ones. For example, the Morrigan can be a potent source of strength and determination for those fighting injustice; but it is the responsibility of the individual to decide what type of weapons and how much force it is ethical to use – and to know when to stop fighting and to seek dialogue before legitimate opposition degenerates into terrorism.

The dialectic between individualism and the requirements for social participation and responsibility is reflected in the characters of the goddesses and gods themselves. In some of the evocations, the archetypal force is directed mainly towards self-realisation, finding one's own true purpose and releasing the creative spirit, if necessary by rebelling against the over-restrictive aspects of society or by breaking the settled pattern of one's life. In other evocations the emphasis is on enhancing the individual's abilities and power to contribute to the establishment of a just and beneficial social order that enables people to live in freedom, peace and harmony.

The needs of society tend to promote stasis: living together requires rules and the means to enforce them. Sometimes the rules are not explicit but are expressed through peer pressure, disapproval and ostracism. The urge towards individualism, on the other hand, promotes movement, seeking the freedom to break the forms, to change, to be free of concern for consequences for others. Each individual seeks their own point of balance between these two poles, but the search for balance never ends as that would lead again to stasis. The balance that is sought is that of the dancer: one moment we are dancing enthusiastically with others, helping to develop forms and rules; the next we are breaking free, off on our own creative adventure.

In calling on the ancient gods, modern Pagans cannot avoid recreating them, seeking ways to make the energies they represent relevant to the issues, stresses and ideals of present-day society. In compiling these evocations, we have selected themes from the rich tapestry of mythology that surrounds all the goddesses and gods included here. Our selection inevitably reflects our current Western European perspective and our own individual predilections. We offer them in all humility but with the belief that, used with positive intent, these evocations can enrich and expand the psyche, allowing previously unrealised inner qualities and strengths to emerge. They tap ancient wisdom that is both within and without, and open up marvellous opportunities for living more fully and joyously.

# *Acknowledgements*

First, I wish to express my appreciation to my husband, Zachary Cox, who wrote nine of the original eleven evocations. His understanding of the essence of the gods and his ability to express it in lyrical prose-poetry are magical and provided the inspiration for the essays, and also the template for the ones that I have added. I am grateful to the many friends who were excited by the original booklet and demanded more, and who have kept me going by asking me when the book will be finished.

Jean M. Williams

# The Gods and Goddesses

# *Aphrodite*

*A*phrodite, the Greek Goddess of Love and Beauty, is one of the most familiar in western culture: Her myths have inspired exquisite works of art from Ancient Greece to modern times. She represents the ideal of female beauty and allure. She is of pre-Hellenic origin, probably a Phoenician fertility goddess similar to Ishtar and Astarte, but her cult spread throughout the Mediterranean and she was adopted into the Hellenic pantheon and integrated into its myths.

Aphrodite was born from the foam of the sea: in the battle of the Elder Gods, Chronos dismembered his father Uranus, and cast his father's genitals into the sea; where they fell, a white foam formed. From this foam emerged a woman of such grace and beauty that all nature rejoiced. She was carried by the gentle west wind Zephyrus to the shores of Cyprus which is regarded as her birthplace; hence she is referred to by Homer as the "Cyprian", an adjective used in the eighteenth century to describe the beautiful and accomplished courtesans often maintained by noblemen of that time.

Aphrodite was a multi-faceted goddess, reflecting the complexity and subtlety of love, sexuality and relationship. As Aphrodite Urania ("Aphrodite of the mountain"), she represented the highest ideal of selfless love; as Aphrodite Genetrix, she protected marriage and helped maidens find suitable husbands; as Aphrodite Pandemos or Porne, she was goddess of carnal love and lust and patroness of prostitutes.

In contemporary western culture, with the sexual freedom that improved contraception has brought, all three aspects of Aphrodite are of extraordinary relevance. Each one of us, both male and female, is familiar with the inner conflicts that arise as we struggle to reconcile and integrate all aspects of love: our ideals of selfless love, our family loves and responsibilities, and our lusts and desires to enjoy our sexuality to the full. The perhaps naive ideal is to find that integration through a relationship with one life-long partner. The high rate of divorce shows how difficult this is.

Aphrodite is Goddess of Beauty as well as Love and the two aspects are intertwined: when we love, we perceive beauty; when we respond to beauty we feel love; and both have an erotic component that is not simply sexual but self-transcending. For foam-born Aphrodite manifests out of the deep ocean of our instinctual and emotional nature and from the depths of the unconscious mind. She is beauty and delight, the erotic Kundalini energy that rises from the root of our being. She awakens all our senses to beauty and pleasure, and enhances our capacity for deep relationship, aesthetic appreciation and creativity.

Aphrodite wears a magical girdle about her waist that gives her the power to speak straight to the heart. It is not through intellect that we meet her but through being open to our feelings and emotions. Aphrodite carries in her hand a Lamp and by its light she enables us to integrate our sexuality with our higher nature and to find our spiritual wholeness. When we surrender ourselves to another in the act of love, we find self-transcendence and discover the god or goddess in our partner.

Aphrodite's Roman equivalent is Venus, who gives her name to the beautiful golden planet most often seen in the western sky shortly after sunset. She is Stella Maris, Star of the Sea. Her Zodiacal influences are connected not only with the development of our sexual nature and relationships, but with our capacity to form and maintain loving relationships with family and friends. All relationships can be enhanced if we seek the goddess or god within the other.

Aphrodite is attracted to and attracts the complementary force of the testosterone male: she is married to the ill-favoured Smith God, Hephaestos and she also has an on-going affair with Ares, God of War. But her effect on these rough, tough males is to evoke their softer side; through love they find their capacity for tenderness and deep relationship. They learn to appreciate and value beauty. From the liaison between the Goddess of Love and the God of War was born Harmonia: through love, strife can become creative and result in a new state of harmony.

Aphrodite is also the mother of Eros, the mischievous god of instant sexual attraction. Those struck by an arrow from his bow may be plunged into painful, conflicting emotions between the new irresistible attraction and their other loves and commitments. Aphrodite has her dark side and her myths vividly describe the jealousy, possessiveness and competitiveness that often cause such pain and havoc in our relationships. The myth of Eros and Psyche is particularly relevant: Eros falls in love with Psyche but is only permitted to wed her provided she never looks upon his face and discovers he is a god. He woos Psyche and she lovingly promises never to attempt to see his face; however, her jealous sisters convince her that her husband must be a terrible monster if she is not allowed to see his face and she agrees to light her lamp after Eros has fallen asleep and look at him. She does so, and sees the beautiful face of the god. In her amazement, a drop of hot oil spills and wakens Eros who immediately vanishes. Heart-broken and ashamed, Psyche searches everywhere for her husband, coming at last to Aphrodite to plead for help. Aphrodite tells Psyche that she must fulfil a number of difficult and humiliating tasks before she can regain her love. The goddess appears stern and remorseless in her jealous vengefulness, but Psyche perseveres, growing in the process towards maturity and wisdom. She is finally reunited with Eros and is accepted into the company of gods as a goddess.

Jealousy, anger and self-doubt are part of the gamut of human emotions that arise within relationships. The myth of Eros and Psyche portrays the often painful process of moving beyond the "in-love" stage, learning to see the other more truly and to love more fully. Aphrodite's Lamp of Wisdom enables us to find our way through the confusing maze of our conflicting emotions. In the process of seeing the god or goddess within the other, we also discover the goddess or god within ourselves and experience true union, the Sacred Marriage. We may then begin to recognise our own unassailable inner beauty and capacity to love and be loved; through this realisation our sexuality is integrated with our spirituality. This is the inner Sacred Marriage.

The evocation of Aphrodite is appropriate in many situations: it may be used simply to affirm the value of sexual attraction and passion, or to enhance one's capacity for love in all relationships, to deepen one's understanding of this aspect of one's nature. It may also be used to seek the guidance of Aphrodite's wisdom in times of stress and difficulty in a sexual or any other relationship. The rays of her Lamp cast light into the dark corners of our emotional nature, allowing us to be honest with ourselves; we learn to see truly what is of value in a particular relationship, to forgive and let go of resentment, and discover hidden and unexpected beauty.

Perhaps the most rewarding use of the evocation is to find that inner sense of beauty and grace, the Goddess of Love within.

# *Aphrodite*

Incense: Benzoin, Rose, Red sandalwood

Hail Aphrodite, Lady of Love and Delight, who art
throned amid the Cypress Groves on the shore
of the Great Sea. From the Lamp in thy right
hand pour shafts of light, pearly and emerald
green. Thou art girdled with roses and emeralds,
fire-opal and lapis lazuli. Thy voice is the Music
of Doves, the Breath of Ecstasy.

Put forth the Magic and Mystery of thy Beauty;
infuse all creatures with thy subtle allure, to
seduce, to intoxicate, to fascinate the soul.
Display by concealment. Initiate by mystification.
Bring us through delicacy to rapture and scented
sleep.

Wherever nerve-ends sharpen to the Kiss of Sense,

Wherever eyes flash to sudden awareness at the
promise of Love,

Wherever the soft, the warm and the fragrant seduce
us from crueller paths,

There falls thy Light.


By the marriage of Spirit and Flesh,

By the Breath of Innocence,

By the delicacy of subtlety,

By the self-transcendence of wantonness,

By the soft caress of the Dove and the sharp caress
of the Serpent,


I call upon thee to Be with Us

in Body and in Spirit.

*Zachary Cox*

# *Apollo*

*T*he Greek Sun God, Apollo, was also called "Phoebus", the Brilliant One. He was not the sun disc itself; that was represented by Helios. Apollo is the light-giving, life-giving power of the sun and carries all the connotations of the Zodiacal Sun and the Sun Tarot card. He was considered to be one of the most important and powerful of the gods. His cult is very ancient and was widespread throughout the Hellenic world from at least the 7th century BCE. His main shrines and places of pilgrimage were Delos, where he was born, and Delphi, the site of his oracle.

His divine lineage was high: he was the son of Zeus, the King of the Gods. His mother was not Zeus's wife but Leto, Goddess of Night: Apollo was Light born out of Darkness. Artemis, Goddess of the Moon, was his twin sister. Apollo's birth was long and difficult due to the jealousy of Hera, the wife of Zeus, who prevented the Midwife Goddess from attending his mother. But when he was born, all of nature rejoiced and a wonderful fragrance filled the air. He was fed on nectar and ambrosia, the food of the gods, instead of mother's milk. He immediately threw off his swaddling clothes and emerged as a beautiful athletic youth on the brink of manhood. In his many statues, he is depicted as beardless and with the long hair of one who has not yet passed through the rites of passage to manhood.

As soon as Apollo was born, he demanded a bow and arrows, which Hephaestos, the Smith God, made for him. His arrows flew to their target with deadly accuracy over great distances, symbolic of the farsightedness and aspiration that the solar light brings. Under his influence, the winged arrows of our thoughts can fly into the future to formulate plans and envision our dreams.

Apollo represents one of the great universal cosmic forces. Like the Sun itself, his power was capable of great benefits and great ills. The myths describe his ruthlessness in pursuing his desires and in avenging himself when slighted. But they also tell of his nobility, his tireless energy and his creativity. He has the well-being of mankind in his hands: he can send plagues and sickness, yet he is also a god of healing. Asclepius, the physician, was his son.

One of Apollo's most important functions was as the god who presided over the oracle of Delphi. The myth recounts that he pursued the serpent Python that jealous Hera sent against his mother, and killed it outside its lair in a mountain gorge at Pythia. The gorge was the site of an oracle of the Earth Mother situated in a cave. Apollo established his sanctuary at Pythia and took over the divinatory function previously attributed to female underworld deities. Its name was changed to Delphi but the presiding oracular priestess was known as the Pythoness. The slaying of Python and the establishment of a solar divinatory function is sometimes interpreted as the light of the higher mind and intellect displacing more primitive instinctive and emotional reactions to events and to the challenge of the future. Nowadays, we have learnt to value both approaches, seeing each as being appropriate in different circumstances. Apollo's priestess, the Pythoness, made divinatory utterances that were often ambiguous and difficult to determine. They can only be interpreted in the light of the higher wisdom.

The Delphic oracle was a source of moral ideas that permeated Greek thought; for example, that killing another required atonement and purification. Apollo himself had to atone for the killing of Python and had to undergo purification. Two sayings express the wisdom and morality of Apollo: "Nothing in excess" and "Know thyself".

Apollo was also the patron of music and poetry and is often depicted holding a lyre. His music brings joy, harmony and healing of the spirit. It is central to his function as a god of healing. His rites included the performance of a "paean", a ritual song and dance in praise of Apollo created for the occasion. The paean was an inspirational rite of praise, thanksgiving and healing. The word has passed into the English language to denote a poetic or musical expression of praise.

Apollo's companions were the nine Muses. Their sweet voices enchanted the gods on Mount Olympus but they were also guardians of Apollo's shrine at Delphi. The Muses inspire the creation of music, poetry, drama, history and astronomy and bring spiritual sustenance and self-transcendence. The muses were all female entities, personifications of idealised inspiration and perfection in creative work. Many artists and poets have found their inspiration in particular women; but both men and women can find their inspirational muse through Apollo.

Apollo's creative inspiration has connotations of intellect and an aesthetic that gives high value to form, skill and perfection, combined with spiritual aspiration. He brings together intellect ("Logos") and the highest level of emotion – pure love, or "Eros". Their synthesis gives rise to a particular wavelength of creative endeavour – poetry, music and art that "sings". The epithet "Apollonian" is used to distinguish this type of creativity from the Dionysian – the more shamanic, earthy and spontaneous approach associated with the god, Dionysus.

Beware how and when you evoke Apollo; his power is very strong and can be heedless of its effects on others. He can give the driving energy that sweeps all before it, regardless of consequences. But called upon after due consideration and with ethical intention, he can ignite the inner creative fire and keep the flame of inspiration burning. He can put you in touch with your inner muses and open up new creative avenues. He can also bring healing by boosting the recuperative powers of mind and body and can restore flagging energy and enthusiasm.

As a divinatory god, he brings clarity of mind and far-sightedness, the ability to transcend the ego and access the wisdom of the higher self in considering future action. It is wise to evoke him before undertaking any divinatory procedure that concerns future plans and aspirations.

Evoke him with a paean of music, dance and poetry.

# *Apollo*

Incense: Frankincense, Sandarac, Rosemary, Bay (for divination)

Hail Apollo, Lord of Light and Life, throned in the Rosy Fire of Continuous Creation. In thy right hand is the Golden Lyre whose music is the Life of the World. About thee, all things revolve in perfect balance. All gods and creatures are thy limbs, thy hands, and thy feet. Thy voice is a rich song, strong and joyous, in which all joys and pains are lost and refound.

Pour out thy bounty, the zest and delicacy and the fierce gentleness of thy song.

Illumine and warm the Worlds, and infuse the soul of man with the Holy Joy of Creation.

Wherever seas flow or winds blow,

Wherever blood flows and seeds ripen,

Wherever Man emerges from his prison to claim the
heritage of eternal freedom,

Thy glance is on the World.


By Art and Light,

By Dance and Joyful Journey,

By the fragrance of Spring and the gold of Summer
and the fountain of Eternal Youth,


I call upon thee to Be with Us

in Body and in Spirit.


*Zachary Cox*

# *Ares – God of War*

*T*his was a difficult essay to write: in common with many western Europeans, I find aggression, conflict and the use of force challenging and uncomfortable. My first reaction is to avoid confrontation, to look for a means of conciliation and compromise. While these are virtues in a civilised society, they can become weakness and an abrogation of responsibility: if one is not prepared to draw a line or take a stand at any point, conciliation can become cowardice and can endanger the very values of freedom and mutual respect that it professes to support. Contrary to expectation, the willingness to stand firm can often cause the aggressor to back down, thus avoiding serious conflict.

Ares was the Greek God of War. Son of Zeus and Hera, he was to his father "the most hateful of all the gods" (*Iliad*). Ares was regarded by the Greeks as an angry, impetuous god and was generally hated and feared, though honoured by all great warriors. His twin sister was Eris, Goddess of Discord; she it was who provided the golden apple that set the conditions for the Trojan War. Ares gloried in war and in all the warrior virtues of valour, skill of hand and eye, strength, discipline and the will to win. He is the Warrior King in his chariot, a leader who inspires loyalty and courage to deal with an outside threat. He was accompanied into battle by his sister Eris and his sons Phobos (Panic) and Deimos (Fear), whose names have been given to the moons around the planet Mars.

There is something both challenging and excitingly glamorous about the archetypal Warrior that evokes a deep response from within the psyche. It is therefore not surprising that Ares was loved by Aphrodite, Goddess of Love, who bore him several children. But Aphrodite was married to Hephaestos, the Smith God. Myth has it that Helios, the Sun God, saw Ares and Aphrodite making love and told Hephaestos, who crafted a net of fine mesh and placed it over the bed. Hephaestos then pretended that he was going away for a few days, but he secretly kept watch. He managed to catch the two naked lovers in the net and called all the gods to come and laugh and jeer at them. It might have been expected that such public humiliation would have led to implacable hatred and feuding. The fact that it did not can only be due to the mediating charm of Aphrodite who seems to have convinced both males that neither had really lost face since both had had the honour of sleeping with the Goddess of Love and Beauty, whom all the gods desired.

In the *Iliad*, Ares fights on the side of the Trojans in support of Aphrodite who had played a significant part in the events that led to the war. She had beguiled Paris, the Trojan prince, into judging her the fairest of three goddesses by promising him Helen, the most beautiful of mortal women, as his wife. Unfortunately, Helen was married to Menelaus, King of Sparta; when Paris eloped with Helen and carried her off to Troy, Menelaus mobilised his Greek allies, vowing that Troy and Paris's entire family would be destroyed. The two goddesses Hera and Athena, who had lost out in the beauty contest, sided with the Greeks. Athena actually wounded Ares at one point, forcing him to return to Olympus to be healed. There were great and noble warriors on both sides and the war lasted for ten years. The Greeks finally won by cunning strategy rather than force of arms and the cost to both sides in pain and death was enormous. For every victory there is a defeat; and every victory is to some extent incomplete, and even the victors always have a price to pay. And from every defeat there are lessons to be learnt.

The Roman equivalent to Ares is Mars. Originally a god of agriculture and fertility, Mars became with time more strongly associated with the requirement to defend one's land and the competitive and aggressive forces necessary to maintain and improve conditions. Mars was the father of Romulus and Remus, the founders of Rome, thus all Romans considered themselves descended from Mars. The empire-building Romans had a greater understanding than the Greeks of the function and requirements of the soldier in human society. Mars was nobler, more idealistic and more disciplined than the aggressive and impetuous Ares. His worship was widespread and he had many temples and shrines throughout the Roman Empire, whereas there were few temples to Ares. The Romans understood that peace and the rule of law could only be maintained if backed by disciplined force. Among the less imperialist Greeks, the role of discipline and military strategy was ascribed to the cool, intelligent Pallas Athena who, as we have seen, sometimes opposed and overcame the God of War.

The planet Mars rules Aries, the first sign of the Zodiac, which the sun enters in March, the month of Mars. Astrologically, the attributes of Mars tend to be seen nowadays as closer to the Greek view of Ares than to the Roman view of Mars: raw, aggressive energy and action, fierce impetuous will, the joy of battle and the adrenalin rush – hugely successful survival traits in a dangerous competitive world. But a constant source of disruption and conflict if not combined with a sense of honour, integrity and justice.

What is the legitimate role of the aggressive, competitive, fighting spirit of Ares/Mars in today's society? When and how should we evoke this harmonic within ourselves?

The Ares force is raw and strong in small children who often have to learn the hard way that angry yelling is not an effective way to achieve their will in a world where the larger person has the power. So the child learns strategies and tactics to achieve goals, and discovers the rewards of love and approval. But so often in our society the child learns that all anger is bad and sinful; the self-motivating energy of fierce will is repressed, leaving us powerless and prone to project our aggression outward, seeing ourselves as surrounded by people and events to fear.

Anger is in itself neither good nor bad but a basic human emotion that fuels action. It is how it is directed and expressed that matters. The wisely reared child learns to discriminate and to evaluate with the intelligent mind. The virtues of Ares are energy, courage and fortitude; the vices are cruelty and tyranny. Anger and aggression are katabolic: by destroying form they release force for action and for the development of new structures. Destruction always brings a sense of pain and loss but also the excitement of new opportunities and new ventures.

Our language recognises that life is in a sense a perpetual battlefield. We speak of battling against cancer, war on want, soldiering on, being fighting fit, fighting the elements. There is an exhilaration in competition, in pitting one's strength and skill against another's or against impersonal forces of nature, in taking risks. There is a zest in joining forces with like-minded people to face a challenge, in putting aside one's own self-centred concerns to pursue some nobler end, some greater cause. Evoke Ares when life seems flat and dull and your energies are low. Evoke him when the challenges with which you are faced seem overwhelming, when you cannot see what role you can play or how you can find the leadership skills you need. Evoke him when an individual or group threatens the rights or liberty of others. Dare the possibility of confrontation, destruction and change.

# Ares

Incenses: Dragon's Blood, Opoponax

Hail Ares, Lord of Austere Courage, who throned
in thy chariot ride ever into the scarlet glare of
battle. In thy right hand is the flaming Sword of
Thought, tempered in Will's fire to serve the
cause of Action. Thou art helmed and girded as
a warrior, thy strong arms girt with studded
leather. Thy voice is the brazen tone of the war-
horn, a shout of exultation, an ineluctable
command, the cry of the wolf, a battle song.

Now shall the Earth tremble and the walls crumble
before thy Warrior Will, before the discipline of
thy Thought, and the hard necessity of thy
Cause. At the end of soft ways, and beyond the
chance of compromise, it is thy power that shall
call the tune, thy fire in the blood, thine ice in
the mind, thy song the Heroes sing.

Wherever Life confronts its own brink, facing
   oblivion with defiance,
Wherever a man carries his belongings on his back,
   and sleeps beneath the stars,
Wherever weathered, narrowed eyes scan the
   horizon for hazards, and the odds of survival are
   weighed, and Life itself is gambled with a song,
There is thy scourge set on the flanks of Life.


By hard rations and hard marching,
By the Nobility of Strength and the unwritten Laws
   of War,
By the spilt blood of Heroes dead and the hot blood
   of Heroes living,
By the jesting oath flung in the teeth of Death,
By the Joy of Victory and the Bitterness of Defeat,


I call upon thee to Be with Us

                              in Body and in Spirit.


*Zachary Cox*

# *Artemis*

*A*rtemis is most clearly an archetype for our time. Although some of her myths express a rather brutal ruthlessness, her essential spirit shines through and has a resonance for many women today. She can be seen as the first feminist: Woman Whole unto Herself, Virgin Goddess, wild, free, beholden to no man.

Artemis was the daughter of Zeus and Leto and twin sister to Apollo, the Sun God. Like him, she was a bringer of light, but hers was the light of the Moon. She is particularly associated with the new moon and is sometimes depicted with a crescent on her brow. At the beginning of the lunar month, her light is seen in the western sky at evening, beautiful, remote but full of potential. Like her, we can each month regain our virginity, our innocence, our sense of self, as she lights our way into the new lunar cycle, filling us with excitement, energy and optimism for the creative opportunities ahead.

When Zeus asked the infant Artemis what gifts she would like him to give her, she asked for eternal virginity, a bow and arrows like her brother's, the office of bringing light, a knee-length hunting tunic, and a retinue of ocean and river nymphs to accompany her and to care for her hounds and stags. She also asked for all the mountains of the world.

She is described by Aeschylus as "the Lady of the wild mountains" and she spent most of her time in mountainous and forested places far from the dwellings of men. She is depicted as a beautiful young woman clad in a short tunic with buskins of soft leather on her feet, carrying her bow and arrows. She loved hunting and the excitement of the chase. But she was also the protectress of animals. She is the wild spirit of Nature; she incorporates the exuberance of instinctual animal life that is born, nourished on living things, grows, mates and dies, often as a meal for another creature. She represents both the hunter and the hunted, the mystery of life feeding on life. Nature is not sentimental or squeamish; neither is Artemis.

In ancient times, the hunting of animals, particularly in the winter months, was essential to survival. Artemis was invoked by hunters to help them find their quarry and for their arrows and spears to fly true to their target. In some parts, her cult involved the sacrifice of many animals and birds to propitiate the goddess and to ensure successful hunting. This practice reflects the feelings of powerlessness that men suffered in the face of the uncertainties of nature which often seemed cruel and capricious. When frightened, the human mind is capable of many crazy ideas and such wasteful death is not in keeping with the true spirit of the Artemisian archetype, for Artemis also presided over the fertility of animals and protected the suckling mothers and their young. Wanton killing for trophies or self-aggrandisement was abhorrent to her.

Artemis loved to dance with her nymphs on the banks of some mountain stream or to bathe in its waters. Her music was the sound of running water, the breeze in the trees, birdsong, the buzzing of insects and the cries of animals. She was no man's plaything. One of her best known myths describes how she was observed bathing naked with her nymphs by young Actaeon: one can imagine the macho wolf whistle that led to his being discovered. Artemis was so angry that she turned him into a stag and his own hounds tore him to pieces. Artemis tolerates no disrespect and deals with men on her own terms. She is assertive, proud, courageous – she knows who she is and what she wants.

Paradoxically, Artemis is also patroness of childbirth. When Leto gave birth, Artemis was the first to be born, quickly and without pain. Leto was then in painful labour for many hours with Apollo and the newborn Artemis was immediately able to help her mother. She thus became the goddess that women in labour appealed to for safe delivery. When, as so often happened, the birth resulted in the painful death of the mother, Artemis would mercifully dispatch her quickly with one of her sharp arrows.

The association of Artemis with childbirth reflects her role as protectress of animals and their fertility. Her intimate familiarity with wild nature makes her a suitable companion at the time of that most animal of women's activities, the bearing, birthing and suckling of children.

At Ephesus, the cult of Artemis centred around her fertility aspect rather than celebrating her prowess as Virgin Huntress; many will be familiar with the statue of the many-breasted Artemis found in her temple there. Yet Artemis was also the patroness of young unmarried girls who danced at her festivals. Artemis affirms the inviolate individuality within each one of us. We are all "whole unto ourselves", responsible for our own life decisions. Whereas Aphrodite urges us towards relationship and reciprocity, Artemis encourages us, even when in relationship or giving birth, to maintain our personal integrity, our self-esteem, our independence of spirit. This is truly to be "ever virgin", whole unto ourselves.

Artemis is energetic, physically fit and active, skilful in the use of the bow. A modern Artemis is likely to be trim of body, to be able to mend a fuse or change a wheel on a car and perhaps to be proficient in a martial art. To Artemis, life is a constantly unfolding adventure, full of interest and possibility. She keeps her innocence and has no truck with cynicism or pessimism.

Her appeal to modern women, still struggling to disentangle themselves from stereotyped gender roles and images, is strong. Women, young or old, maiden, mother or crone, can all be empowered by evoking the qualities of Artemis within themselves.

But men also suffer from gender stereotyping and have a dread of being seen as effeminate if they soften the macho masculine image. They are exhorted to acknowledge their feminine side but are not given an acceptable idea as to what this means. Artemis provides an image of the feminine that carries none of the connotations of weakness and dependency so prevalent in the usual stereotype. She challenges men to relate to women on equal terms, with respect and without preconceived ideas. Through her, men also can discover their inner integrity and be whole unto themselves. They can then dare to approach Artemis as Goddess of the Moon to find the key to their sensitive and imaginative creative depths, so often inaccessible to the stereotypical male.

To both men and women, of all ages and situations, the evocation of the Artemisian spirit can bring liberation into one's inner core of personal integrity.

# *Artemis*

Incense: Lignum Aloes, Copal

Hail Artemis, Virgin Huntress of the Night, who art throned upon the high hills in the silver light and indigo shadows of the risen Moon. In thy right hand is the Bow, and in thy left hand the leash of thy Hounds. On thy feet are the buskins of soft leather, and thou art crowned with the Crescent Moon. Thy voice is a bell of clear command, not to be gainsaid.

Swiftly and surely weave thy way among the shadows of the Soul's Night; Mistress only of thyself, yielding to none, pursue thy native way. Thy shafts strike silver fire from the Earth. Thou art ever on the horizon, ever remote, nor Man nor God may possess thee; yet thou art at the centre of all creatures, the Foundation of the Worlds of sense and dream.

Wherever tendon and muscle stretches to the athletic stress of joyous effort,

Wherever Woman strides unveiled and armed, her own Mistress,

Wherever heads are high and eyes alight with the Fire of Freedom,

Wherever hair flies in the wind,

There is thy footfall heard among us.

By the tireless pursuit of the Quarry,

By the Rhythm of the Endless Chase,

By the compulsion of dreams and the restless tide of the future,

By wayward will and ready hand,

I call upon thee to Be with Us
in Body and in Spirit.

*Zachary Cox*

# *Athene*

*W*ith a shout of triumph, Athene sprang fully formed and fully armed from the head of Zeus, and all the gods were filled with awe at the bright clarity of her grey eyes.

Her mother was Zeus's first wife, Metis, whose name means wisdom. It had been foretold that if Metis bore a son, he would surpass Zeus in power; so when Metis became pregnant, Zeus swallowed her and her unborn child. Zeus then developed a terrible pain in his head; to relieve his agony, Hephaestos clove Zeus's head with a bronze axe.

It is as though Zeus himself suffered the pains of labour in order to give birth to a more focused aspect of himself. This emanation of Zeus is female – a most redoubtable goddess, combining warlike strength with wisdom.

Athene is depicted wearing a helmet, sometimes with snakes round the brim; she carries a shield and a spear; on her breast she wears an aegis. The aegis is thought to be a protective leather breast covering made of goatskin, with a Gorgon's head in the centre. Athene is also portrayed with an owl, a bird that was used to represent her on coins.

Her myths are numerous and sometimes conflicting, reflecting the antiquity and wide geographical spread of her worship. She is of pre-Hellenic origin and it has been hazarded that she may have developed out of the Minoan snake goddess cult that existed in Crete a thousand years before the Hellenic period.

The myths surrounding her role as the Patron of Athens are the richest and most relevant for us today. It is told that she vied with Poseidon, the God of the Sea, to become Patron of Attica. Each gave a gift to the people of Athens who were requested to judge which was the most acceptable. Poseidon gave the gift of a well of salt water, but Athene gave the olive tree. She won the accolade of the people since the olive is not only the source of a nutritious fruit, of oil for lamps and for cooking, and of beautiful wood for carving; it is also a symbol of peace. Athene is often depicted with an olive branch in her hand.

Her name sometimes bears the prefix, "Pallas", which means "Maiden". She was a Virgin Goddess and defended herself vigorously against the aggressive amorous advances of Hephaestos. Her qualities are of the mind rather than of the body. She personifies forethought and the self-discipline of pleasure deferred in order to achieve specific desirable ends. She is credited with introducing many crafts and skills: the taming of horses, boat building, architecture, the potter's wheel and the crafts of spinning, weaving and embroidery – all technologies that require skill, effort and the imagination to envisage a beneficial end product.

The snake theme sometimes present on her helmet and clothing and the Gorgon on her aegis can be interpreted as the instinctual nature kept under control by self-discipline. She is not primarily concerned with control of the sexual instinct but with taming the instinct towards aggression and violence. Athene herself shows this reaction when she loses a weaving competition to the girl Arachne and spitefully turns Arachne into a spider. But in general her myths are refreshingly devoid of the human failings shown by most of the Olympian gods.

Athene is the goddess of civilised living. The words "city" and "civilisation" both have the same Latin root. Civilisation is about learning to live together in large groups for mutual benefit. It involves defining roles, accepting differences, making and abiding by rules, establishing a set of common values and a climate of mutual respect. As a warrior, Athene protects the city from invaders but she also keeps the peace within the city. For, inevitably, when large numbers of people live together, there will be angry disputes, clashes of interests, differing values and priorities. Athene has the power and the weapons to quell civic unrest and the wisdom, mediation skills and sense of justice to sort out the conflict so that understanding and harmony can be restored.

Athens was the birthplace of democracy – an infant form compared with today's more sophisticated versions: neither women nor slaves were permitted to vote in ancient Athens. Nonetheless, it was based on a vision of an ideal social order far in advance of its contemporaries and, indeed, more civilised than many regimes today. The way of a tyrant is to impose his will and his own view of what is "right" by force. In a democracy there is discussion and debate, a chance for different viewpoints and interests to be expressed in order to reach a consensus or to agree a compromise for the general good. Athene presided over the first tentative steps towards using means other than force to establish a peaceful and prosperous society.

Athene represents the highest ideals of social cohesion and co-operation. When things go wrong and people's expectations are disappointed, when there is injustice and gross inequality, the natural reaction is anger. But expressing anger usually in turn triggers an angry response, and the confrontation escalates. This is part of human nature. We see it at every level from families to villages to cities to countries and on the international scene. Athene brings qualities of cool appraisal, wise understanding and the gift of skilful communication to try to resolve confrontation and dispute.

Conscious awareness that angry confrontation results only in more angry confrontation is far from widespread: a lot of wasted energy and grief could be avoided if people understood this and were more willing to accept Athene's olive branch.

Anger is a very powerful emotion and arouses our aggressive instincts. It tends to flare up instantaneously when something goes wrong. Under its impetus, our immediate reaction is to justify our own attitudes and actions and to find ways to blame and condemn those of other people. Thus the conflict begins. Athene teaches us to step back and to view the interaction more dispassionately. Her wise owl whispers that perhaps the actions of the other person were not motivated by malice or selfishness but by perfectly valid considerations from their perspective. Then instead of reacting angrily, we might ask the other why they behaved as they did. Then we can learn to take a wider perspective that encompasses the needs, fears and expectations of others as well as our own or those of our family, group or nation.

Most importantly, we can begin to see our own role in the development of any conflict situation in which we find ourselves, even if it was only a lack of awareness of how people were feeling. Then we can move away from the "Who's to blame?" mentality to a view that sees the conflict as arising out of a series of decisions and actions by the parties concerned, all taken for reasons that seemed good from a particular perspective. From this comes understanding and the notion of shared responsibility rather than blame. If no one has to be made to feel guilty, there is a chance for mutual forgiveness and reconciliation. This was the process so brilliantly put into operation by the Truth and Reconciliation Commission in South Africa to heal the wounds of Apartheid.

Athene is not afraid to fight when necessary. She wages war against tyranny and denial of human rights; but she has the wisdom to realise when the fighting should end and the process of constructive peace-making should begin.

Athene has a half-sister, Eris, Goddess of Strife and twin to Ares, God of War. It was Eris who threw down the golden apple in front of Hera, Athene and Aphrodite, an act that led to the Trojan War. Eris provokes conflict, but conflict is not necessarily negative: it may be painful but it provides the impetus for change and growth. What is important is how we handle the energy of the anger that conflict arouses: we can use it to empower our self-justification and desire for victory and revenge, or we can use it to wake us up to the need for change, to shake us out of our complacency and to find out how the conflict arose. We can then move rapidly on from our anger to the constructive process of seeking mutual understanding and the creative give-and-take that can resolve the conflict productively.

The qualities that Athene can bring are clearly of great value when strife arises. We can evoke her power within ourselves to help us find the wisdom and objectivity to resolve conflict and to play a creative role in bringing about reconciliation and change. We can wear upon our breast the protective aegis that covers our heart, arm ourselves with the Spear of Will and hold out the olive branch of peace. But we can also use the evocation to empower ourselves in a more general way in our daily lives, to become firmer, fairer, wiser and more principled in all our social interactions.

# *Athene*

Incense: Frankincense, Galbanum, Sage

Hail Athene, Goddess of Wisdom and Will, who springeth fully armed from the forehead of Mighty Zeus. Thou art throned in the noble City where men and women dare to speak freely. Thou art the Virgin Mother of Liberty. On thy head is the Helmet of Wisdom, on thy breast the Aegis of Invulnerability. In thy right hand is the Spear of thy Will and in thy left hand is the Olive Branch of Peace.

Let thy spear ever be ready, Lady of resolute courage. And let the Lamp of thy Wisdom shine forth that True Will may be illumined and guided by reason.

Wherever there is the Will to stand against tyranny,

Wherever War gives way to Reason,

Wherever Peace is founded on Courage and
Wisdom,

We have seen the glint of thy Spear.


By the mysterious Owl, wise bird of night,

By the graceful Olive, tree of patience and peace,

By the sharp pointed Lance, symbol of True Will,


I call upon thee to Be with Us

in Body and in Spirit.


*Jean M.Williams*

# *Dionysus*

*D*ionysus is a dangerous god, yet to ignore him is even more perilous.

He represents the wild side in the constant struggle for balance between control and freedom from restriction. Too much control of impulses and emotions is stifling, stultifying personal growth and creativity, resulting in a drab, gray, unsatisfying life. The Dionysian force within the psyche is very strong; if denied expression, it may break through in destructive uncontrollable ways, as outbreaks of rage, violence, rape, alcoholism, panic attacks, even psychosis.

But evoked with an open mind and heart, Dionysus can be a god of transformation, enabling us to break the fetters of outmoded attitudes and habits, taboos and inhibitions. The longer and more firmly we have held on to these fetters, the more destructive and disruptive their breaking may seem, to our own lives and the lives of others. Yet it can clear the way for creative change into greater freedom and harmony, and ecstatic union with the life force.

Dionysus gave the gift of wine to humankind and his rites and myths reflect the contradictions and paradoxes of its use: in moderation, conviviality, euphoria and the gentle release of inhibitions; in excess, uncontrolled wildness, violence, sexuality and the obliteration of the everyday functioning personality, followed by a clouded memory of what one did. Dionysus could be loving and gentle or aggressive and bloodthirsty.

The worship of Dionysus is ancient and gradually spread throughout the Mediterranean wherever the vine was cultivated, from Turkey in the east to Rome in the west, where he was known as Bacchus. As his cult spread, he often subsumed the qualities of the local deities of agriculture and viticulture; his character and myths were enriched in the process. He became a god of pleasure and patron of certain aspects of civilised living such as theatre and music.

He is thought to have reached the Greek mainland about 800 BCE and accounts of his birth were assimilated into the Olympian mythos. He was the son of Zeus and Semele, a mortal woman. The pregnant Semele was persuaded by jealous Hera to demand that Zeus show himself to her in his full glory as he would to a goddess. Reluctantly, he did so and Semele was consumed by the burning fire of his majesty. The premature babe was saved and placed in Zeus's thigh from which the child was born in due time. He was thus known as "Twice Born".

Some of his festivals may have been simple celebrations of the grape harvest or of the maturation of the new wine, similar to many festivals still held in the wine-growing areas of Europe. Others in the earliest times may have been violent and excessive, even involving human or animal sacrifice. But in later centuries, especially in Athens, they took on the characteristics of a shamanic mystery religion, his worshippers entering a state of ecstatic possession through the ritual use of wine, drumming and dance: "Entheos" (having the god within) is the root of our word "enthusiasm". His rites were celebrated in wild places, away from towns, and were "orgiastic" in the true sense of the word ("orgia" meaning a sacred rite).

The ritual use of any consciousness-altering drug can have a quite different effect from its recreational use. Context and intention have a profound influence, bringing about "Entheos", a state of self transcendence that unites the human and the divine within, to be truly "twice born" into a new dimension of the psyche. The celebrants in the rites of Dionysus were often inspired with the gift of prophecy. His worship was associated with Delphi before the advent of

Apollo, and Dionysus ruled Delphi for three months each winter while Apollo visited the Hyperboreans in the far north.

Euripedes' play *The Bacchae* powerfully dramatises the consequences of trying to suppress the Dionysian force. When Dionysus arrives in Thebes, Pentheus, the king, has him captured and imprisoned, hoping to suppress his unruly worship; but chains cannot hold the god and the doors fly open. Dionysus leaves the town and goes up into the hills, followed by his worshippers, the Maenads, among whom is Argave, the mother of Pentheus.

Pentheus is infuriated by the flouting of his authority, not only by his prisoner but by his subjects, including his mother, who choose to follow the god into the wilderness. He decides to follow them to discover what goes on in their rites. He disguises himself but is of course spotted because Pentheus is incapable of dancing or letting himself go. The Maenads, in the grip of ecstatic frenzy, tear him to pieces. The myths say that he was mistaken for a wild animal and that the rites of Dionysus involved the tearing to pieces of an animal, eating its flesh and drinking its blood, which were thought to be the flesh and blood of the god. When Argave finds out in the morning that she has taken part in the slaughter of her own son, she is distraught and after burying him she goes into voluntary exile in expiation.

The conflict portrayed in this horrific tale is apparent every day in our newspapers: on the one hand, bigotry, self-righteousness, fundamentalism and the repression of women, on the other, drunken violence, rape, drug addiction, vandalism and crime. The teenagers taking ecstasy at a rave are seeking something that is missing in their lives which they see as drab and lacking any sparkle of creative opportunity for enthusiasm. The drug is well named; ecstasy is a fundamental human desire and there are so few legal or socially approved ways to obtain it. The revivals of shamanic practices in Pagan paths and in some of the Christian churches are attempts to find a safe route to ecstasy.

Euripedes' play is a cautionary tale, not an example of how to counterbalance repression and restriction in the modern world. There are subtle inner ways to release one's Dionysian spirit without causing social or psychological havoc. That is the objective of the evocation which follows. Dionysus is the Lord of the Dance: he represents that precarious balance between apparently irreconcilable opposites that can only be achieved by dance, the balance between spontaneity and forethought, instinct and reason, wildness and civilization. He treads the fine line between our reasoned thought structures and mental habits by which we construct the world in which we live, and the freshness of perception and imagination that we had as little children. In adult life, those who have lost touch with this childlike way of experiencing sometimes regain it through psychedelic drugs or psychosis, dangerous ways that can lead to loss of the ability to function in the everyday world. By imagery and language, this evocation aims to unlock the door between sane, rational thinking and the inchoate yearnings of the unconscious mind, out of which wells a wild creative energy and enthusiasm, a source of new ideas, insights and inspiration.

Use the evocation with or without a glass of wine, with or without music, in stillness or in dance, alone or with friends. Capture the results in picture or poetry. Celebrate the dance of the god-spirit within.

# *Dionysus*

Incense: Musk, Frankincense

Hail, Dionysus, Lord of the Dance, Fruit of the marriage of Earth and Heaven, who art throned amid the vineyards in the light of the Sun. Thou art crowned with ivy and garlanded with roses. In thy right hand, the pine-cone-tipped staff calls forth the Joy of Being. Thy left hand crushes the purple grapes to yield the dark Wine of Ecstasy.

Tread thou the edge of the precipice between Reason and Unreason, Bringing gifts of mystery and terror. Only thou, in thy divine madness, art able to reconcile Order and Chaos, Freedom and Law, Repression and License, Adventure and Security – Sanity and Madness. Through thee shall we regain our innocence.

Wherever Spirit rebels against the Grey Enemy,
Wherever Mystery is more seductive than
Certainty,
Wherever the dark reaches of the Psyche cry out for
expression,
Wherever the yearning for the heights of ecstasy
nourishes the Soul's wisdom,
Wherever the Wine of Life flows to excess –
Thou art there, where the Dance is wildest.


By the phallic power of the Sun and the scent of
the Rose,
By the holy intoxication of spirit and flesh,
By wine and dance and the beat of the drum.
By the Light of the Black Diamond in which form
is unmanifest,


I call upon Thee to Be with Us
in Body and in Spirit.


*Jean M.Williams*

# Hermes

*H*ermes is the Greek God of ... what? Now you see him, now you don't. As with the metal Mercury, (the name of his Roman equivalent), he slips from our grasp, changing and assuming a multiplicity of shapes.

His essence is speed. He is depicted as a lithe, athletic young man with a winged hat and wings on his sandals. He carries in his hand the Caduceus, a staff with a winged top and two snakes entwined around its shaft, symbolic of the paradoxes and complementary nature of opposites: good and bad, truth and lies, joy and sorrow, male and female.

The main source of the best-known mythological stories about Hermes is one of the Homeric Hymns, written in the sixth century BCE but referring to a much earlier age. It tells that Maia, Hermes' mother, was the daughter of the Titan, Atlas. She was wooed by Zeus and gave birth to Hermes in a cave in Arcadia. He grew with miraculous speed into a little boy, eager for adventure. He left the cave and travelled far and fast. He came upon a herd of cattle that belonged to his half-brother Apollo, and decided to steal some of them; so, when night fell, he crept among the herd and separated out about fifty cows. To escape detection, he disguised the trail by making shoes of oak bark and plaited grass for the cows' feet. The ruse worked and Apollo searched long and far for his cattle but could not find them. Hermes meanwhile had returned to his cave where he fashioned a lyre from a tortoise shell, on which he played beautiful music that lulled his mother to sleep. Apollo had offered a reward for finding the thief of his cattle and was finally directed to the cave. He woke Maia and demanded the return of his cows that her son had stolen. She pointed to Hermes, feigning sleep in his swaddling clothes, and said, "He's only a baby!" But Apollo seized Hermes and took him to Olympus and charged him before Zeus with theft. Hermes confessed, but played such beautiful music on his lyre that all the gods were enchanted. Apollo immediately wanted the lyre and offered Hermes the herd of cattle in exchange, which Hermes gladly accepted. The two brothers became friends from then on.

Zeus was impressed and amused by Hermes' daring, ingenuity and eloquence and made him his herald and messenger, giving him the winged hat and sandals for speed of travel and the Caduceus staff as the symbol of his office. The herald was an important official at the court of the king in Ancient Greece, responsible for the proper conduct of ceremony, ritual sacrifice and divination by lottery. Oaths were sworn on the herald's staff and his staff was placed between warring factions to stop fights. His person was sacred and inviolate. Roman ambassadors seeking to negotiate a peace treaty carried a form of this caduceus. Hermes was no simple carrier of messages: he was a magician and priest, and a consummate diplomat and negotiator, dispatched to resolve disputes or to persuade people to a particular course of action in accordance with the will of Zeus.

Zeus gave Hermes responsibility for making treaties and contracts and promoting commerce, activities that involved travel; Hermes therefore also became responsible for the maintenance of rights of way for travellers. And so Hermes' sphere of influence spread: he became the god of commerce and the market place, and the guide and protector of travellers. Pillars of stone or "Herms" were placed at boundaries, crossroads and divisions of the way. By extrapolation, he was also the messenger for Hades, guiding souls to the realms of the dead; he guided Orpheus to the Underworld to find Eurydice.

Hermes' cheeky theft of Apollo's cows resulted in him being regarded as the god of thieves and liars; but he also promised Zeus that he would protect property – perhaps the origin of the adage, "Set a thief to catch a thief". His thieving is not petty: it is the exercise of guile, stealth and trickery for a joke – how could a newborn babe steal a herd of cows from a god? Only by magic and cunning. It is the archetypal story of the little kid winning out over the big guy.

Hermes was also associated with Aphrodite in ritual practices for the making of love charms. He gave Pandora the gift of subtlety and feminine wiles. It seems that the arts of seduction were associated with the guile and subtle cunning of Hermes as much as with the charm and beauty of Aphrodite. Hermes even seduced Aphrodite with his golden tongue, and she bore him a son, Hermaphroditus, who combined the qualities of both.

The symbolism of the Caduceus with its two snakes entwined about a staff is very old, originating in Mesopotamia and associated with the goddesses Tanit and Ishtar. It was also found in ancient Egypt, associated with the god Thoth, who has many of the characteristics of Hermes. Out of a synthesis of Greek, Egyptian and Arabic learning came the study of alchemy and what became known as the Hermetic Tradition of magical study. Many of the greatest and most inventive scientists of the Middle Ages and the Renaissance worked within this tradition; their symbol was the Caduceus; there is thus a long-standing association of Hermes with scientific experimentation and discovery.

Hermes also became a god of craftsmen. Hephaestos was the god of the magic of metalwork, but Hermes made the lyre and the panpipes that produced the magic of music. He also gave mankind fire-sticks as a way of making fire.

In the Tarot, Hermes is associated with the Magician in the Major Arcana. He has command of the four Elemental weapons and is Master of Magic. He is a guide to our own inner pathways, giving sudden clear insights and the realisation of new exciting possibilities. He helps us to integrate all aspects of the Elements. But he is also a gambler and illusionist, god of the casino and the stage magician. We must be prepared to take chances, to seize the opportunities that appear to arrive by sheer luck, to accept good fortune, but beware of the excesses that Hermes can so easily lead us into.

Hermes is the god of a particular aspect of intellect and an aspect of Zeus. His primary gift is clarity of mind – that quicksilver speed and precision of thought that identifies similarities and differences, that categorises and organises information, that measures and quantifies. He also gives the gift of eloquence and persuasiveness. He is the god of language and communication. He manifests in the scientist who spearheads innovative research and communicates the results clearly; and in the brilliant barrister who marshals the facts and then presents his client's case; he is in the skilled negotiator in politics, industrial relations and conflict situations. He is the god of computers, the Internet and the World Wide Web.

Hermes retains certain child-like qualities: curiosity, impulsiveness and a sense of mischief, but combined with a very adult quick-wittedness and ability to size up a situation. He can cause division and argument as well as talk people into agreement or joke them into forgiving laughter. He is the god to evoke when tempers are getting frayed and people are beginning to take up intransigent positions; Hermes will find a way to reduce the tension and restore a sense of humour and a broader perspective.

His golden tongue and quick wit can also be used for ignoble ends: he can be seen in the confidence trickster, the advertiser that makes misleading and exaggerated claims, the journalist who twists the truth to make a story, the gossip who spreads rumours, the hacker and the virus writer. Hermes is ever the Trickster and needs to be kept under the control and guidance of Zeus.

At the highest and most fundamental level, Hermes is that aspect of the evolutionary force that seeks expression in ever-greater complexity of organisation, which ultimately manifests in the development of mind. He is the creative, syntropic life force that counterbalances the inherent entropy of the universe. It is serendipitously appropriate that the spirals of DNA, the building blocks of life, so closely resemble the entwined snakes of the Caduceus.

Astrologically, the planet Mercury has all the attributes of Hermes, both noble and ignoble. The evocation presented here aims to help one align oneself with and strengthen the positive Mercurial qualities within the psyche. As herald and messenger, Hermes is a facilitator; he facilitates the smooth running of commerce and the legal system; he facilitates peace talks; he facilitates travel and movement. He invents the lyre and gives it to Apollo to facilitate the Sun God's music and poetry. He facilitates communication of every sort. He brings order out of chaos; he can also bring chaos out of order, to break outmoded systems and to make way for new forms to emerge. He brings flexibility, lateral thinking and innovation. His evocation can be used to enhance his qualities of intellect, organisation and communication within the psyche in general, or to help prepare one to deal with a particular situation or solve a particular problem.

# *Hermes*

Incense: White Sandalwood, Storax, Sandarac

Hail Hermes, Lord of Mind, swift jesting Messenger, in endless flight through the orange and violet Aethyr. In thy right hand is the Serpent Wand of Science, Magic and Healing. Thy winged feet are set upon the clouds, and wings crown thee. Thy voice is laughterful as living water and clear as the stars.

Divide the Light from the Darkness, the North from the South, and flash as quicksilver through the veins of the Universe, bearing the Divine Word.

Wherever atoms dance or planets whirl,

Wherever the Syntropy of Life turns back Time's
Arrow,

Wherever Form crystallises from the Void,

Wherever the Mind of Man razor-cuts toward Truth,

Thy Voice is heard.


By the Double Helix of the Seed of Life,

By the Miracle of Language,

By the Joy of Swiftness and the Laughter of the
Endless Quest,


I call upon Thee to Be with Us

in Body and in Spirit.


*Zachary Cox*

# *Magna Mater*

*T*he archetype of the Great Mother Goddess is universal. She is found in Pagan religions from antiquity to the present day and in all parts of the world. She is known by many names but all recognise her as the Great Mother. To some, she is cosmic: the feminine creative source of the manifest universe – the stars, the sun and all its planets. To others, she is the Earth Mother, source of life on Earth. In this collection of evocations, we have selected Nuit to represent the cosmic feminine; the evocation of the Magna Mater expresses the qualities of the Earth Mother, but in the last part of the evocation there is recognition that Life itself is cosmic. Since the basic elements of life are present even in the furthest stars, the potential for life exists throughout the universe.

The Great Mother as Earth Mother is well represented by the Greek goddess, Demeter, mother of Kore, the Spring Maiden who became Persephone, bride to Hades and Queen of the Underworld. Demeter gave the gift of grain to humankind and taught them agriculture and animal husbandry. Her name means "Corn Mother"; whereas Gaia is the

Earth itself, Demeter is the fertile soil upon it. She is the goddess of the cultivated countryside, of herds and flocks, of fields full of golden wheat, of trees and vines laden with ripening fruit. Her blessings are fertility of all creatures, human and animal, the nurturing of the young, and the abundance and beauty of flowers, lush fields and flowing streams.

Our hearts open to her as to our own mother; we feel ourselves surrounded by the comfort, security, unconditional love and generosity of the good mother. We respond with our love and gratitude for the good things of life – and with appreciation of the amazing beauty of this planet that is our home.

But Demeter loses her beloved daughter; the Flower Maiden of Spring is stolen away by Hades. Demeter's grief and fury are terrifying, threatening all life with famine and disaster. She is finally placated by a compromise solution agreed before Zeus: Kore will spend nine months of the year with her mother on Earth, and three months of the year below with Hades as Persephone, Queen of the Underworld.

In her grief, Demeter was said to have taken refuge in Eleusis, about 22 kilometers from Athens, and every autumn, when Persephone left her again, Demeter returned sadly to Eleusis to await the return of her daughter in the spring. Eleusis became the main centre of her worship and the twice-yearly Eleusinian Mysteries became famous throughout the Greek and Roman world. They are thought to have originated in Mycenean times, 1500 years BCE, and continued until Christianity became established.

The Eleusinian Mysteries were celebrated at the time of the sowing of the wheat in October, and also in February, when the dormant seed sprouted and the first green shoots appeared. The autumn rites were the more important and every five years a major nine-day festival was held in September, involving a processional pilgrimage from Athens to Eleusis.

Although the Eleusinian festivals were public celebrations, only initiates were admitted to the secret rites within the great temple of Demeter. Initiates swore an oath not to reveal the content of the rites, an oath so effective that to this day the details of the rites are unknown. What is known is that there was a probationary grade and a full initiatory grade, the full initiates having access to a deeper level of mystery. There is much speculation as to what happened in the rites: it is known that sacred objects were carried in procession from Eleusis to Athens and back again; it is thought that these were probably farm implements, symbolic of the great gifts of Demeter to humankind. The rites for all initiates probably included an enactment of the abduction of Kore, Demeter's grief and search, and the final return of her daughter, bringing life back to the earth. The inner rites, for full initiates only, may have included an enactment by a priest and priestess of the sacred union (hieros gamos) between Demeter and Zeus that led to the birth of Kore.

The essence of rites of sacred mystery is that they are mysterious – beyond rational description and explanation. It may well be that the effectiveness of the oath of secrecy sworn by initiates was because the rites themselves, when described to a non-initiate, seemed quite simple, but that the actual experience was so profound that it was beyond words. The rites involved days of physical, mental and emotional preparation, including fasting; initiates were admitted to inner parts of the temple, normally seen only by priests and priestesses. Everything was designed to create a numinous atmosphere, a context in which the rites would have a deeply spiritual effect.

The whole mythos of Demeter and Zeus, Hades and Persephone concerns the mystery of life and death and renewal, the bounty and also the harshness of Nature and the gods. An inscription found at Eleusis and comments made by Greek writers who had experienced the rites indicate that an outcome of the experience was an intuitive grasp of the mystery of life and death and an acceptance of one's own mortality.

"Beautiful indeed is the Mystery given us by the blessed gods: death is for mortals no longer an evil, but a blessing."

Inscription found at Eleusis

"Thrice happy are those mortals, who having seen these rites depart for Hades; for to them alone is granted to have true life there; to the rest, all there is evil."

Sophocles

"Happy is he who having seen these rites goes below the hollow earth; for he knows the end of life and he knows its god-sent beginning."

Pindar

The story of Demeter and Persephone is an allegory of the cycles of Nature. The Great Mother brings forth her flowers and fruits in their due season. She is patient and accepts the time required by the natural processes of gestation and birth, whether the birth of a child or the birth of an idea. Hers is the deep wisdom of Life itself.

For present-day Pagans, the myth has a special poignancy. It reminds us that events are not always under our control: the familiar cycle of the seasons is subject to greater cycles that we know little about and that can be disrupted by apparently random events. Climates evolve and change; the Earth is restless; earthquake, storm, flood, and forest fire are natural phenomena. The Great Earth Mother is not just the mother of humankind but of all life on earth. She is the life-process of the planet itself.

Demeter gave special gifts to humankind – agriculture and animal husbandry – that led to better nutrition and more free time to engage in activities other than finding food. Living in co-operative groups, arts and crafts and the appurtenances of civilisation followed. Humans multiplied and filled all corners of the earth, a process that has escalated in the last two centuries to an astonishing degree. During this period human knowledge, technology and communications have also taken an amazing leap forward. While all this is part of the life-process of the planet, it is now seen as being at the expense of other parts of the life-process.

With special gifts come special responsibilities. It is time for humankind to become the grown-up children of the Earth Mother, putting aside adolescent irresponsibility and heedless greed. Surely the Great Mother weeps now for the alienation of her human children, the desecration they have brought to her fields and forests, lakes, rivers and oceans, to the very air she breathes. But humanity is part of Nature, part of the body of the Great Mother. We can see ourselves as that part of her that reaches towards self-awareness, towards imagination, foresight, intellect, aesthetic appreciation – a reaching that manifests not only in science and technology but in poetry, philosophy, great literature, civilised laws and the organisation of great cities. It is also expressed in the ways we co-operate with the rest of Nature in agriculture, gardening, conservation work – in the way we stand aghast at the harm we have done to the Great Mother and thus to ourselves.

This evocation captures what we believe to be the essence of the Mysteries of the Great Mother; it is a celebration of Life in all its wondrous variety, an expression of love and gratitude, an affirmation of hope and trust in the future, an acceptance of our place in the cycle of life and death and renewal. We evoke her exuberant generosity, her love and caring, and her fecundity, within ourselves.

# Magna Mater

Incense: Dittany, Storax, Benzoin

Hail Great Mother, Queen of Flowers and Fruitfulness. Thou art throned in sacred groves concealed within the green valleys where men build their homesteads. Thy robe is green as the Summer meadows, and gold as the ripening corn; and in thy right hand is the diamond sceptre that forever renews the Clear Light even in the darkest places of Earth. Crowned art thou with roses and honeysuckle, with violets and vines and the leaves of the oak; and within thy body sleeps the Secret of the Future; and thy voice a deep bell sounding in the Soul of Man, that is the Call of Love.

Pour out thy Joy, that all Life may share in this Sacrament of Bliss, that Eternal Ecstasy, the Kiss of thy Lover, the Lord of Light.

Wherever a flower lifts to the sun, and the fruit
   grows heavy on the tree,
Wherever the voices of children rise in gladness,
Wherever Action springs from the Ground of
   Love,
There is thy gracious presence manifest.


By the steady measure of the Timeless Dance,
By the Joy of Union,
By the scent of bread new-baked, and the taste
   of honey,
By the Mystery of Life ever renewed in the
   Womb of Eternity,


I call upon Thee to Be with Us

                              in Body and in Spirit.


*Zachary Cox*

# *Pan*

*I* hesitated to include an evocation of Pan in this collection. I could not hope to emulate the power, passion and poetry of Aleister Crowley's magnificent *Hymn to Pan*. But the collection would be incomplete without a tribute to this great archetypal force that is much loved by, and relevant to, modern Pagans.

Pan was not one of the Olympian gods who were part of the complex civilised life of the city states. He was located in rural Arcadia where the people were farmers and hunters. He was a spirit of Nature and the god of fertility of crops, animals and people.

Half-man, half-goat, he has the upper body of a man but his head has the horns of a goat and his lower half has a goat's shaggy legs and hooves. He has a goat's sexual appetites. He is the wild god of the woods and hills. His name means "All" and he represents the primal life force. His titles were "Pan Phage, Pan Genitor": "All-Devourer, All-Begetter". In colloquial parlance, "Eat anything, fuck anything". He combines the destructive and the creative aspects of Nature, the exuberant, burgeoning, competitive, lustful, joyful, irrepressible energy behind evolution and the proliferation of life on this planet. He is sexual, sensual, seductive, untamed and amoral. He calls to our animal nature that we have been taught to repress and control to the point where we lose touch with it and fear it. Pan has an irresistible and thus terrifying attraction for us. We fear his physicality, his unashamed indulgence in, and enjoyment of, instinctual appetites.

Pan cut and bound together seven reeds of different lengths to make the first pan-pipes, with which he made wild and seductive music. He seduced many nymphs with his music and fathered many children. It is said that he alone was able to bed Artemis, Virgin Huntress of the Moon, Woman Whole unto Herself. Only straightforward sexuality, uncompromised by "civilised" notions about gender roles could attract her.

His worship was of ancient origin in Arcadia but, in the centuries preceding the Christian era, it became more widespread. It was adopted in Athens and spread to Rome where he was known as Faunus. When Christianity became established, and especially when it introduced a celibate priesthood, the untamed blatant sexuality of Pan became associated with the Devil. Nothing makes sex so tempting and obsessing as shame and celibacy. Country folk, however, could not afford to ignore sexuality: the fertility of their crops, flocks and herds, and of the animals they hunted, depended on it. The worship of the Horned God in one form or another, including the sympathetic magic of making love in the fields at sowing time, persisted in many country places throughout Europe until recent times.

We know that becoming human and civilised requires self-restraint, consideration for others, notions of "the common good". Irresponsible sexuality, rape or the generation of babies without heed for the consequences are not acceptable. But the efforts of humankind to become civilised have all too often gone to the extreme of joyless repressiveness. Pan is the natural enemy of puritanism, of anything that denies and devalues physical pleasure and condemns joyousness and fun.

Perhaps the civilised Athenians turned to Pan because they felt they were getting too dissociated from their sexual nature. This is certainly one reason why modern Western peoples feel such a yearning for him today. So many taboos surround sexuality and sensuality from early childhood in our society that we have difficulty in allowing ourselves to experience our own lustiness, or to confront it in our partners. We become embedded in notions of gender roles and idealised images of how we should think or feel or look or act. We shower, depilate and deodorise ourselves to avoid anyone smelling our lustiness, then perfume ourselves with products sold on the promise of getting the perfect deodorised partner. The greater degree of sexual freedom experienced today has brought a whole new set of complications and problems, exacerbated by marketing and the media. There are many difficulties and dilemmas to be confronted as we seek to reclaim our Pan energy and to integrate it with our aspiration to become fully civilised.

But Pan himself is half human and half animal and also a god. There is no need to fear that the animal will overwhelm the human. He represents balance and integration.

We evoke him to rediscover the natural spontaneous life force within ourselves, the simplicity of our animal nature, to take pleasure in it and to respect it; to regain our physical heritage of lusty enjoyment of all aspects of life; to value our bodies as they are, without constant self criticism; to accept fully all our bodily functions without shame or disgust. Through finding this unashamed, life-affirming impulse within ourselves, this Pan-nature, we also come to accept it and welcome it in others.

The evocation of Pan helps us to balance the human and the animal and become whole. He enables us to escape the pressures of modern living that sometimes make us feel that our heads are about to burst. He puts us in touch again with our physical bodies so that the tensions that have built up are released. We forget for a while how we look and enjoy how we feel physically instead. We dance freely to his music, play games, find that almost any physical activity can be enjoyable if done with zest. Through Pan, we find a new dimension to our sexuality.

# Pan

Incense: Pine (wood or resin)

Hail Pan, wild Goat God of Arcadia, half man, half goat – all beast yet all divine. Thou art throned amidst thyme and rosemary on the rocky hillside. We see thee nimble-footed on the dizzying heights, leading the flock to fresh pastures. Thou art crowned with horns, and in thy hands are the seven-reed pipes. Thy voice is the wind in the trees, the pulse in the blood, the laughter of the amorous chase.

Play thy wild sweet music in the woods and on the hillside, to seduce us from the wearisome and the negative. Breathe into us your animal energy and fierce joy, the wisdom of the body triumphant.

Wherever a glance kindles the fire in the heart,

Wherever a voice, a touch or a perfume stirs the
blood,

Wherever prudence gives way to joyous adventure,

Thy pipes are heard, and the drum-beat of hooves;

And thy breath is felt on the neck.


By the hot pulse of passion shared;

By wild music and joyous abandon;

By lust and love and laughter


I call upon thee to Be with Us

in Body and in Spirit.


*Jean M.Williams*

# Persephone

*P*ersephone was the Spring Maiden and yet also Queen of the Underworld. Her mother, Demeter, was one of the ancient great Mother Goddesses from pre-Olympian times, associated with fertility, abundance and the arts of agriculture. Demeter was brought into the Olympian mythology as the sister of Zeus but kept her independent status; she had no consort but mated with whom she chose. Her daughter was, to begin with, simply called the Kore (the Maiden) and represents all young, fresh, innocent life.

One day, the young Kore was picking flowers when suddenly the earth opened and Hades, Lord of the Underworld and brother to Zeus, emerged in his chariot and snatched her up. Her cries went unheard and she was carried off to the Underworld where she became his bride and his Queen. In the Underworld, she became Persephone, "She who brings destruction" (in Rome, Proserpina, "The Fearsome One").

Demeter was distraught with grief at her daughter's disappearance. Although she searched everywhere she could find no trace of the girl, but the crops withered and no fruit was set on the trees as Demeter neglected the earth's fertility, and focused all her energies on the search. After many days, Demeter came to Helios, the all-seeing Sun God, who told her that he saw Kore abducted by Hades. In a rage, Demeter travelled to Olympus and demanded that Zeus summon his brother Hades to return her daughter to her. Concerned for the survival of humanity and all life on earth, Zeus agreed that Kore should be returned, provided she had eaten nothing in the Underworld. Hades was summoned, together with Persephone, and appeared before Zeus; but it was established that Persephone was seen eating seven seeds from a pomegranate. Thus Hades claimed her as his consort and Queen. Demeter declared that she would not lift her curse from the earth unless her daughter was returned to her. Zeus exerted his kingly power and proclaimed a compromise solution: that Persephone will spend three months of every year in the Underworld as Queen, and will then return to her mother and become Kore for nine months. (In northern Europe, where winters are longer than in Greece, we have tended to amend this to a six-month cycle.)

This is one of the best-known and richest archetypal stories of ancient Greece. It became the basis of the Mystery cult of Eleusis, which celebrated its rites in the spring and autumn for many hundreds of years. The rites included an enactment of the myth but the central mystery was shrouded in secrecy. It is apparent that the autumn rites in particular were of an initiatory nature, intended to be a life-changing experience of spiritual rebirth for the participants.

The myth can be understood on many levels. The most self-evident concerns the mystery of the changing seasons: thankfulness for harvest, the mourning of the passing of summer, the planting of seeds and the celebration of returning life in the Spring; also the paradox of the uncertainty of the weather within the predictable rhythm of the year. The significance of agricultural implements in the Eleusinian Mysteries may have been designed to raise awareness that humankind has to work with the forces of nature to grow crops and raise animals and that we are dependent on its rhythms.

The myth also explores the mystery of life and death. Many ancient myths recount how the goddess goes down into the Underworld in order to confront death. Here, Death snatches away the young maiden and all the Earth mourns until she is returned. It is an attempt to understand why there is death. Hades is "The Ruler of Many and the Receiver of Many". All, it seems, must eventually enter his realm. But there is also the miracle of new life in a great cycle of Life and Death and Renewal. In contemplation of this cycle, boundaries dissolve to be replaced by a sense of the oneness of all life, an awareness of being part of a great and wonderful whole, the great dance of life and death.

This myth also contains a more personal inner significance. On Earth, Persephone is the Kore, a child; but in the Underworld she is a formidable Queen ("She who brings destruction") and the wife of Hades. Here is a portrayal of the transition from the innocence of childhood to responsible maturity and sexuality through confrontation with the inner darkness, the darkness of the unconscious mind and the shadow self. Within that darkness are hidden all those parts of ourselves that we do not wish to acknowledge: our basest and most untamed instincts; all those aspects of our human nature that we despise and fear; all those hidden thoughts and feelings incompatible with the idealised image of ourselves that we want to project. By going down into our own Underworld and accepting all of ourselves as fully human, we release the creative energies of the unconscious and achieve formidable royal stature.

At the deepest level of all, the myth depicts the sacred marriage of the goddess and god within, the integration of all aspects of the psyche deep within the Underworld of the unconscious. As Persephone returns each autumn to her husband in the Underworld, so we continually seek to reach new levels of integration. It is a never-ending journey, but as Spring ever returns, so do we also emerge from the darkness, strengthened and renewed.

This evocation touches all these levels. Persephone is presented as Goddess of Transition, She who stands at the Gate between the Worlds. She can be evoked for meditation on the seasons or to celebrate Spring or harvest time; or to help deal with the sadness of loss of a loved one, whether human or animal; or at times of transition in one's life, especially when that urge towards growth and integration arises from within, demanding maturity, strength, and willingness to change.

# *Persephone*

Incense: In her dark aspect: Poppy seeds, Myrrh
In her spring aspect: Copal, Dittany

Hail Persephone, Goddess of the Gates of Death and Life, who art throned in the midst of a Spring garden in the shadows of the Underworld. In thy right hand is the deadly fruit of Hades, the pomegranates whereof all creatures must eat at the last. Thou art crowned with calm leaves, and with poppies and corn. Thy voice is a low call heard at evening, luring the hearer to deep dreams.

Wait then eternally at the Gate between the Worlds, that there might be a sweet grave welcome for Life as it passes into Death, and a light, swift welcome for death as it passes into Life; for at every Spring shalt thou return to us, and gladden the Earth with birdsong, and

cleanse eye and mind to innocence, that a new
tale may be told.


Whenever Sleep follows Waking and Waking follows
  Sleep,
Wherever the Rhythm of Days and Seasons call forth
  an echo from the souls of creatures,
Wherever Life passes from Flesh to Earth to Flower
  to Flesh,
It is thy Garland that is worn, thy Saraband that is
  danced.


By the Brevity and the Eternity of Life,
By the Pulse of Light and Darkness,
By the Seed hidden under the Ice,
By the shed skin of the Serpent,
By the Hope that is beyond Hope and Despair,


I call upon Thee to Be with Us
                    in Body and in Spirit.


*Zachary Cox*

# *Zeus*

*Z*eus is the king of the Olympian gods and represents all kingly virtues. Astrologically, he is associated with the planet Jupiter, named after his Roman counterpart. His zodiacal influences are concerned with successful participation in society.

The myths describe how Zeus replaced the Elder Gods by overthrowing his father, the Titan Chronos. It had been foretold to Chronos that he would be killed by his own son; to avoid this fate he therefore swallowed each of his first five children as soon as they were born. Rhea, his wife, was determined to save her sixth child and gave birth secretly in a cave, giving the child, Zeus, into the care of nymphs. She then wrapped a stone in cloth and gave it to Chronos who swallowed the stone. When Zeus grew to manhood, he went to the Titans' court and became Chronos's cupbearer. With the aid of Rhea, his mother, he gave Chronos an emetic drink so that he vomited up the stone and the five children that had been swallowed. Zeus then led his brothers and sister in rebellion and the Titans were cast out.

The Titans were cruel and primitive: Zeus brought a new and more civilised regime based on the rule of law. It encompassed the natural laws by which the universe operates and also the necessary rules that allow a society to function harmoniously. The natural laws must be recognised, accepted and worked within. The rules appropriate to a good society have to be based on the human ideals of justice, compassion and wisdom. Zeus represents these ideals. He is the good and noble father.

Although Zeus was the youngest, his brothers and sisters chose him as leader because of his kingly qualities. True authority is not dependent on seniority or status but on courage, wisdom and a proper sense of self-worth. The evocation of Zeus enables us to tap these qualities in ourselves.

Zeus recognises that not only does he have power over those he rules but that with power comes the responsibility to protect and nurture his people. How often do the captains of industry remember this? Without this realisation, power becomes tyranny and despotism.

Many people who find themselves in a position of authority, at work or in other areas of their lives, have difficulty in asserting themselves in a positive way. Some resort to bullying or arbitrary control mechanisms, "pulling rank" or constantly quoting rules and regulations; others feel inadequate and simply evade confrontation, desperately afraid of making themselves unpopular. It is no wonder that leadership and assertiveness workshops are so numerous.

Zeus is charismatic: he has the leadership qualities that inspire enthusiasm and co-operation. Because he has nobility and integrity, he is trusted to be working for the common weal. He exemplifies the effective and gracious exercise of authority.

A "position of authority" usually carries a title: queen, foreman, manager, school prefect, captain, teacher, etc. But all of us from time to time find ourselves in social situations that have no formal structure yet require someone to take a lead: a group of friends trying to decide how to spend an evening; someone falling ill at a party; an amateur dramatic society getting itself organised – there is a wide range of possible scenarios. If no one is prepared to be the first one to make a suggestion or express an opinion, everyone becomes uncomfortable and embarrassed and time is wasted. Holding within ourselves a little bit of the leadership and assertive qualities of Zeus can help us to be effective in many social situations. Zeus is not a warlord; he does not grab at power and want to take charge of every situation. He was chosen by his peers because of his inherent nature. The fear of being thought bossy or domineering is a great inhibitor of effective interaction.

The myth of Persephone shows that Zeus administers justice by listening impartially to both sides. He does not leap to conclusions on the basis of one person's presentation of a complaint but insists on hearing what all parties have to say. His justice is tempered with mercy and frequently results in a creative compromise where both sides give a little in order to receive something of what they think is their due. He portrays the wisdom that comes from taking the broader view, considering all sides of a problem and the larger context in which it occurs.

Zeus also gives generously of himself and his largesse. He is expansive, lusty and zestful, sensual and appreciative, enjoying the good things of life. He will bring himself down to the human level to have a good time and to give a good time. His myths describe his many affairs with both goddesses and human women and he fathers numerous children, many of whom have heroic qualities. He could not appear to mortal women in his full glory as it would destroy them. So, he wooed Leda in the shape of a swan, he came to Danae as a shower of gold, and appeared to Europa as a great white bull. Beauty, generosity and strength can win many hearts.

Zeus has his throne in the high place, at the top of Mount Olympus, and in his hand he holds the thunderbolt, a symbol of power and destruction but also of light. He is a god of inspiration and far-sightedness who will destroy what stands in the way of beneficial progress. Destruction is nearly always painful to someone and a truly Olympian wisdom is required to balance the cost of change against the benefits it is designed to bring.

Like most of the Greek gods, Zeus is capable of rage when his authority is challenged or when he is unable to have his way, which sometimes happens because he himself is bound by the laws he has made. The negative aspects of Zeus result from too much emphasis on his power, resulting in autocratic behaviour, ruthlessness, rigidity and self-importance. The evocation is designed to balance his qualities harmoniously by eliciting his wisdom, compassion and sense of fun as well as his leadership qualities.

Evoke him to find the king within you, to increase your sense of stature and inner majesty, to find the assertiveness and strength to handle situations where you need to take charge, where you need to make judgements and choices that affect others. Evoke him to find his wisdom, power and generosity of spirit.

Feminists may argue that this is a very male view of power, and it is true that the Greek myths have their roots in a patriarchal age. But we live in a society that is still largely structured in a hierarchical way and women increasingly hold positions of authority in which their performance is often judged by traditionally male criteria. If the exercise of authority is dubbed a "masculine" trait, then women need to acknowledge and cherish their inner "masculine" strengths. The archetypal truths embodied in the myths of Zeus are relevant to everyone. Women, perhaps even more than men, can find this evocation empowering.

# *Zeus*

Incense: Cedar wood, Frankincense

Hail Zeus, King of the Universe, Bestower of Realms, throned in purple majesty in the pure soft blue of Empyrean. In thy right hand is the royal orb of amethyst, but thy left hand wields the thunderbolts of Law. The jewelled heavens are thy crown, and thy feet are set upon the mountains and the cities of the Earth. Thy voice is the laughter of great storms, the laughter of great seas, the deep notes of a mighty organ.

Issue then the Word that turns the Wheels, that spins the Worlds and measures out the seasons. Set the Game in motion, order the Endless Dance and pour out the treasures of the universe in a measured and ordered festival of joy.

Wherever a creature rests at ease,

Wherever the Realms prosper,

Wherever there is feasting and music and the
generosity of goodwill, just laws and happy
chances,

Thine hand is felt in the World.


By the Cedar and the Thundercloud,

By the Orb and Sceptre of Imagination Triumphant,

By the Joy that Wills Eternity,


I call upon Thee to Be with Us

in Body and in Spirit.


*Zachary Cox*

# *Bast*

*T*he cat is surely the best-loved animal among modern Pagans, and Bast is one of the most beloved of Egyptian goddesses. Reproductions of the cats of Bast are widely available. They range from regal seated cats, fifteen inches or more high, to small, more realistically proportioned figures. They are often placed in personal shrines and revered as representations of the goddess herself, though more properly they are her sacred animals. The larger statues usually have a golden collar about their necks, a golden scarab on their breasts, symbolic of the Sun God Ra, and some have real gold earrings and nose rings.

The lore of Bast is as complex, confusing and enigmatic as the nature of cats. Her worship was already ancient by the time of the Old Kingdom (around 2500 BCE). There are several variants of her name, reflecting her different centres and the 3000 years of her worship: Bast, Bastet, Ubasti, Pasht, are the most common. According to the Egyptologist Wallis Budge, she was first worshipped in the form of a cat and was probably the patron deity of a town or district. At some time during the Old Kingdom she came to be portrayed as a lioness-headed woman similar to Sekhmet. But whereas Sekhmet wore red, Bast was depicted in green. She was "The Lady of the East", associated with the dawn aspect of the sun when its heat is mild. Sekhmet is the fierce destructive heat of the noonday sun; Bast is its gentle fructifying heat and light that encourages germination, growth and healing.

Sekhmet and Bast are both aspects of Ra, the Sun God; but their powers are complementary: Sekhmet protected the Pharaoh in battle and brought him victory; she thus features as an important goddess on the monuments that record the Pharaohs' lives and exploits. Bast's role, on the other hand, was more generally protective and nurturing, qualities of less significance in terms of rulership; she is thus mentioned less frequently than Sekhmet in the texts. Only one Pharaoh, Sheshonq I (10th century BCE), gives her prominence in the records: he came from Bubastis in the Nile delta, the main centre of Bast's worship. His name is found inscribed on a colossal cat-headed statue of Bast. He reunited Upper and Lower Egypt after a period of schism and disorder, following which Bubastis became the capital of Egypt and the worship of Bast spread throughout the country, remaining immensely popular for the last thousand years BCE.

A magnificent temple was built for Bast at Bubastis (originally "Per Bast", the House of Bast). Here she resumed her cat form, becoming a slim and lissom woman with the head of a cat. Bast is usually depicted with a sistrum in her right hand, a musical rattle also sacred to Hathor with whom she shared a joy in music, dance and revelry. Many sistra have been found, often with a figure of a seated cat at the top. With her left hand Bast holds an aegis to her breast, a semicircular breastplate surmounted by a cat or lion head, symbolic of protection. Many figurines show her with cats or kittens at her feet.

Bast was a goddess of the people rather than of the priesthood, who did not regard her as one of the High Gods; her powers were seen as particularly relevant to the concerns of the home and everyday family life. Large statues of her are few, but there are many thousands of small statuettes and amulets of Bast and her cats in bronze and faience. It is evident that she became a favourite deity of the general population.

All cats, whether in the temple or the home, were revered as sacred. When they died, they were deeply mourned and were frequently mummified and buried in large cat cemeteries. Sometimes the mummified bodies were decked with jewels and supplied with mice for food in the afterlife. Cat mummies were also found in the tombs of their human families. Hundreds of thousands of mummified cats have been found by excavators, so many that a shipload was sent to England in 1890 to be sold as fertiliser.

Wanton killing of a cat was punishable by death, and history relates that a Roman soldier who killed a cat was lynched by a mob. However, many of the mummified cats had been killed by having their necks broken. It is probable that they were sacrificed to Bast since it was common practice to sacrifice sacred animals to their gods. Given the Egyptian view of the afterlife, they may have been sent to the other world with a petition to the goddess.

Bast was the daughter of Ra, the Sun God, and in both her leonine and her cat form represented part of his all-seeing fiery nature. Cats' eyes are highly adapted to see in a very dim light; Bast is thus the Eye of Ra during the night hours. Her eyes change with the light levels, reminiscent of the phases of the moon, which was also regarded as the Eye of Ra at night. In some writings, Bast is the mother of Khonsu, the moon god.

Myth has it that Ra sailed his celestial boat across the ocean of the sky during the day; at sunset, his boat entered the portals of the Underworld. Every night, Ra had to contend with the forces of chaos and darkness in the form of the mighty serpent, Apep. To fight the serpent, Ra changed himself into the tomcat, Mau.

Cats have the reputation of killing snakes and scorpions, which were prevalent and greatly feared in Ancient Egypt. But it was as killers of vermin that cats made themselves indispensable: they were kept in the temples, on the farms, in the granaries and in the home – wherever food was stored. The name, Bast, means "Tearer" and she protected the home, preserving it from thieves (whether human or animal) and from all hidden dangers.

Cats are extremely fertile and noisy in their lovemaking; they are also efficient and devoted mothers. Bast was thus also a goddess of sexuality, fertility and childbirth. She became one of the goddesses of the birth house and many amulets bear prayers or spells concerned with safe delivery of a child or the healing of women or children. One statue is inscribed, "May she grant all life and power, all health and joy of heart".

Cats are playful, charmingly interactive with humans, always lithe and graceful, sensuous, responsive and alert. They have the ability to relax totally and yet to become fully alert in an instant. They are small enough to sit on one's lap, to be stroked, to play with children; yet they are always independent in attitude and manner. They can inexplicably vanish from sight and as suddenly reappear, nonchalantly licking their coat as though they had never left. They are intrepid defenders of themselves and their place: they can fluff themselves out and arch their backs to make themselves look twice their size, and they can yowl and hiss alarmingly.

Small children sometimes exhibit the same charm, spontaneity and interactive playfulness as a cat and little girls were often called "Mai-Sheri" (Pussy).

Bast is a model for any woman who wishes to develop her sexuality, sensuality, social charm, flexibility, capacity for motherhood, yet retain her independence of spirit. The Greeks identified her with Artemis, "Woman Whole unto Herself". But Bast is less of a rebel against the conventional roles of women as wives and mothers, and decidedly more sexual, nurturing and pleasure loving. In many ways she has more in common with Aphrodite.

Herodotus, the Greek historian, visited Bubastis in the fifth century BCE and wrote a vivid description of the magnificence of the temple complex of Bast and of her festival, held in April/May. He recounts that people came by boat in their thousands, playing musical instruments, singing and exchanging ribald jokes and gestures with the people on the banks. It is said that more wine was drunk during the days of her festival than in the whole of the rest of the year.

Bast is not a goddess of the intellect but of the emotional and sensual nature. She puts us in touch with the wisdom of the body, celebrating its physicality. She teaches us to dance the dance of life on swift light paws. Evoking the cat within can enrich men and women of any age. Cats are by nature fastidious and clean, always well groomed, naturally graceful and elegant. Bast can lead us, not just to take more care over appearance, but to discover an inner gracefulness, subtly changing our posture and gestures.

Cats are full of apparent contradictions: capricious yet constant; aggressive yet soft and playful; active and energetic yet able to relax and sleep for hours; tough yet delicate; sociable yet independent; their paws can be gentle or armed with sharp claws, and can strike with the speed of lightning; they are ruthless and efficient hunters, taking live mice back to their kittens to teach them how to hunt; (playing with their prey is a left-over kitten-trait); their voices can be an ear-splitting yowl, a menacing hiss, an attention seeking miaow, an enquiring "prrp?" or a peaceful and soothing purr. Cats look us straight in the eye; they search our faces and our body language, being quickly perceptive and responsive. The human who can call on this variety of qualities with the flexibility of a cat is indeed blessed by Bast.

Bast can enable us to enjoy being alone, to be emotionally and physically self-sufficient and relaxed. But, above all, evoking the inner cat can help us in virtually every type of inter-personal situation. Bast enables us to become alertly perceptive and responsive, assertive yet sensitive and delicate. She teaches us to be firm with children yet loving, tolerant and responsive to their moods and hurts. In the birthing chamber she helps us be relaxed and accepting, rejoicing in the wonder of new life. Bast can help us to find the most appropriate voice and stance to use in any situation. She is the essence of personal charm yet can in an instant transform into a formidable adversary – and equally quickly restore charm and good humour.

Evoke the cat within yourself and imagine your cat-self dealing with the main situations and people in your life. Be prepared to surprise yourself.

# Bast

Incense: Red sandalwood, Benzoin, Musk

Hail Bast, Lady of grace and beauty, Mistress of the Light and the Dark, who art the Eye of Ra in the places of night. Thou art throned in the splendour of thy great temple and in the heart of every home. Thy right hand shakes aloft the sistrum, calling us to dance and joyous laughter. Thy left holds the aegis of protection to thy breast and around thy feet kittens play. Thy voice is the yowl of defiance, the croon of pleasure, the deep purr of delight and intimacy.

Come then on silent feet, Oh Huntress of the Night, stalking the small and timorous fears that nibble away our soul's nourishment. Let all evil and venomous creatures beware thy sharp claws. Yet art thou also our companion by the hearth, the bringer of solace, the healer and comforter.

Wherever the body is alive to sensation and pleasure, and every moment of life is lived to the full with zest and courage,

Wherever women give birth in joy and hope, and children laugh and play,

Wherever the softness of fur and the rhythmic sound of a purr bring cessation of grief and effort,

Thy voice is heard and thy presence felt.

By soft fur and sharp claws,

By pricked ears and tail held high,

By grace and charm and delicacy,

By the mystery of night and the glory of the new day,

I call upon Thee to Be with Us

in Body and in Spirit.

*Jean M. Williams*

# *Nut*

*N*ut is one of the great Mother Goddesses of Ancient Egypt and one of the primal deities of Egyptian creation mythology.

Atum, the first manifestation, arose out of the Waters of Chaos but was passive and inert, a lonely and distressing state. The creative urge arose within him and he spat or (variously) masturbated, and created his son, Shu, and his daughter, Tefnut. Shu was light and air; Tefnut was moisture, gentle rain and soft winds. Shu and his sister-wife Tefnut gave birth to Geb, the Earth, and Nut, the Sky.

The Earth formed the body of Geb and was called "The House of Geb". From his body grew trees, plants and crops, and the dead were laid in their tombs within his body. Geb was one of the gods in the Judgement Hall of Osiris. He watched the weighing of the heart of the deceased and played an important part in deciding whether a soul would be permitted to escape from Earth and journey onwards. The deceased says in the *Book of the Dead*, "My father is Geb, my mother is Nut".

Nut was the sky within which clouds form and the Sun travelled by day. She was also the night sky, full of stars. She was the boundary between the manifest universe and the Waters of Chaos from which the universe emerged; she therefore maintains and protects the universe.

Nut is often represented as a slender woman arched over the earth, her body supported by her fingers and toes which rest upon the earth at the cardinal points. Frequently her body is shown spangled with stars. Geb is sometimes represented as a man, occasionally ithyphallic, lying beneath her. During the day, Shu (Light) comes between Geb and Nut, separating them and allowing the Sun God Ra to sail his boat across the sky. Solar discs, or the Boat of Ra itself, are often depicted as travelling over her body and in one myth Nut is described as giving birth to the Sun every morning and swallowing it at every sunset. Nut "formed the celestial Nile whereon the Sun sailed in his boat" (Budge).

At night the light withdraws and Nut and Geb become lovers. From their union came the High Gods: Osiris, Isis, Set and Nephthys. Nut is referred to as the Mother of the Gods: Geb says, "You are indeed a daughter more powerful than her mother, O Great One who has become the Sky! … You have filled every place with your beauty, the whole earth lies beneath you, you have taken possession thereof."

Nut becomes visible at night, her body shining with a myriad stars. Whose heart has not lifted and opened in astonished adoration at the sight of a starry night sky? It draws out one's soul in wonder and exaltation. It seems the ecstatic culmination of all things.

The Ancient Egyptians believed that Nut's help was essential in the afterlife, enabling the soul to journey through the Tuat in safety and to be reborn as a shining point of light in the starry heavens. She features prominently in the *Book of the Dead* with many prayers asking for her care and protection. She is portrayed as the loving and compassionate mother who gives nourishment and strength for the soul's journey. She was also painted on or inside the lids of sarcophagi, her starry form stretched protectively over the body of the deceased. As the Sun is reborn every morning, so the soul is reborn into a new body of light and into limitless eternal life.

There is occasional merging of the iconography of Nut with that of Hathor, another of the three great Mother Goddesses. Nut/Hathor are both sometimes depicted as a great star-spangled cosmic cow giving nourishing milk to the deceased. They are also both represented as leaning from a sycamore tree presenting water and bread to the soul as it starts its journey in the afterlife.

We can share with the Ancient Egyptians an emotional and spiritual response to the awesome spectacle of the night sky; but, although the Egyptians were diligent observers of the stars over many centuries, modern astronomy has added a new dimension to our perception of the Body of Nut. Now, we are aware of the unimaginable distances between stars, that the stars are also suns that may support other worlds, that there are millions of other galaxies, each containing millions of stars, and that within the Body of Nut there are both entropic decay and disintegration and syntropic creation and growth.

Nut is the Goddess of Infinite Possibility. For the Egyptians, she gave the glorious possibility of eternal life. For us, she expands our physical, mental and spiritual horizons and lifts our imaginations to the stars. She draws us out of our humdrum lives, to lift our heads and raise our eyes to the skies, to look beyond our normal boundaries, to excite us, to exhilarate us, to kindle new hope and new aspiration.

This evocation, by Zachary Cox, was inspired not only by Ancient Egyptian mythology and iconography but also by Aleister Crowley's visionary experience of the goddess Nuit in the Egyptian desert in 1904. This experience found initial expression in the first part of the *Book of the Law*. Crowley later incorporated the final part of his visionary experience of the manifestation of Nuit into his Gnostic Mass, a beautiful and profound ritual that provides an opportunity for all to experience the touch of Nuit. Nuit calls to those who aspire to her with a divine love that is both erotic and cosmic – the marriage of Earth and Heaven, the mating of Geb and Nut, from which we are born as high gods.

Nut is an initiatory goddess, opening the closed doors of the psyche to reveal unexpected vistas, vistas of challenging beauty and mystery that call to our inner depths. The boundaries between Self and Not-Self dissolve in gnosis of the Divine Love that permeates all creation.

Evoking Nut changes our perspective: our attention is raised from personal worries and problems to the limitless creative power of the universe. She is empowering, not through strengthening one's own will and life force, but through connection to and alignment with the positive syntropic forces of the creative divine spirit that permeates the universe. Turn to her when problems seem to press in upon you, when there seem to be few solutions available. Or simply evoke her when the glorious night sky sucks out your soul.

# *Nut*

Incense: Benzoin, Jasmin

Hail Nut, Lady of the Stars, Goddess of Infinite Space, whose Body encircleth the Universe. Thy Body is an infinite Arch of Love, yet thy feet and thy fingers crush not a petal nor a stem of grass. Thy dark body is naked, yet richly clad with a countless multitude of Living Jewels. Thy Jewels are Suns, and the Life of a myriad worlds is lost in that Immensity. Thy voice is the endless music of the crystal silence of the Stars.

Thou art beyond action and inaction, beyond the Steps of the Dance: yet is every Act a Caress of thy Body, every Event a Play of thy Love. Because of thy stillness, thou art a participant in every movement. Each act of atom or brute or man or star pours back its life into thy still, continuous orgasm, and so conceives another Child of Endless Possibility.

Wherever Entropy and Syntropy weave their Endless Dance,

Wherever Two become Naught or Naught becomes Two,

Wherever the Fires flow between the atoms, creatures, souls and stars, all joy and pain, all life and death, all victory and defeat, are alike the Perfume of thy Breath and the Timeless Rapture of Thy Kisses.

By the Wheels of Cosmic Fire which are lost in thine Infinity,

By the secret Serpent Fire which rises in us to aspire to thee,

By the Ultimate Permissiveness of thine Infinite Possibility,

By the Bliss of the Eternal Dance of Stillness,

I call upon thee to Be with Us

In Body and in Spirit.

*Zachary Cox*

# Sekhmet

"Mighty Lady", "Lady of Flame", "Mistress of the two Lands", "She whose essence is Fire": these are just a few of the many epithets of Sekhmet, the lioness-headed goddess of ancient Egypt. Her name means "Powerful One".

She is usually depicted as a black-skinned woman with the head of a lioness. Her dress is red; she holds an ankh in her right hand, symbol of eternal life; in her left, she holds the papyrus sceptre of power. Her headdress is the uraeus serpent surmounted by the solar disk, both symbols of rulership.

Sekhmet represents the blazing heat of the noonday sun in the desert. Appellations such as "Mother of the Gods" and "Lady of the place of the beginning of time" indicate that her worship is very ancient, actually predating that of her "Father", the Sun God, Ra. She is thought to have originated in the Sudan where lions were numerous. As the ancient Egyptian civilisation became more sophisticated, developing a complex social structure and the technology of irrigation, it is probable that lions moved north, inhabiting the borders between cultivated land and the hot and arid desert.

An alternative theory is that she originated in Libya, which, at the time of the dawn of Egyptian civilisation, was more savannah-like than it is today, and probably supported herds of grazing animals – suitable lion food.

As Egyptian society became more centralised, many myths of local gods and goddesses were gradually woven together by the theologians of the Old Kingdom. The ancient Egyptian civilisation lasted 3000 years: although it was in many ways remarkably stable during much of this time, the myths about the gods and goddesses inevitably changed and evolved: god-forms merged and became more complex. Often different forms became complementary aspects of the same underlying principle. The ancient goddess Sekhmet was placed in the pantheon of High Gods that emerged more than 4,500 years ago, when the Pharaohs of the Old Kingdom were starting to build the pyramids. She was positioned as the daughter of Ra, the all-powerful, all-seeing King of the Gods.

Sekhmet represented the devouring, destroying power of the sun's heat, rather than its nourishing, fertilising warmth. She was the active principle that carried out the will of Ra. He placed her on his brow in the form of the uraeus as the "Eye of Ra"; in this form, she was his protectress, spying out his enemies with her far-sight, and destroying them by spitting her fiery darts at them. The Pharaohs identified themselves with Ra; thus Sekhmet was also their protector, especially in battle. She was the destroyer of the wicked and the protector of the good. Some pharaohs described themselves as "Son of Sekhmet".

The violence and destructiveness of Sekhmet is not as a rule indiscriminate or chaotic: in the same way that the lioness fights whatever threatens her young and kills only for food, culling the weaker animals in a herd, Sekhmet destroys that which threatens progress or is weak or out-moded. She is part of the driving force of evolution.

Sekhmet was the wife of Ptah who, at the time of the Old Kingdom, was the great Creator God. She is described as "Greatly beloved of Ptah, Lady of Heaven, Mistress of the Two Lands". As the centuries passed and the centre of power shifted from Memphis to Thebes, Ptah was superseded as Creator by Amun and Ptah became the god of craftsmanship; he was often depicted with a potter's wheel. In this context, Sekhmet still remained the fiery force of will that brings creative inspiration into manifestation. Both Ptah and Sekhmet were very greatly revered during the time of the New Kingdom (1500–1000 BCE), as this was a period of unparalleled craftsmanship. Around 600 statues of Sekhmet were found in the Temple of Karnak, near Thebes. Many of these were carved during the reign of the Pharaoh Amenhotep III (1390–1352 BCE). Thirty-six of these statues are now in the British Museum. There are at least as many in the Louvre. Whatever one may think of the morality of removing such works from their country of origin, it is as though Sekhmet has reached out her paw and her fiery breath to the damp and chilly realms of northern Europe. Some of the statues show her throned, others as standing. The majority are larger than human size and are awesome in their majesty.

As "Lady of Pestilence", Sekhmet could both cause and cure plagues and sickness. We have seen the same apparently contradictory powers attributed to Apollo: the heat of the sun is a powerful force that can bring both great good and great ill. As "Lady of Life", she was mistress of healing and the art of surgery. Because of this, her priests were skilled physicians and surgeons.

One of the most famous Egyptian myths illustrates dramatically how two very different goddesses can be seen as complementary aspects of the same force: it was recounted that the gods learned that humans plotted to overthrow and replace them. Ra was angered by this ingratitude towards the gods who had done much for mankind, and called upon the High Gods to smite them. Hathor, the beautiful goddess of fertility and love who wore the ears and horns of a cow, changed into Sekhmet, a raging lioness, and attacked them without mercy, killing many and drinking their blood. She became so intoxicated with battle lust that human survival was endangered. When Ra saw that she could not be stopped, he became alarmed and sent for beer and certain mind-altering plants. From these a brew was made and coloured with red ochre; it was poured onto the fields where the raging lioness would pass. Sekhmet drank the brew, thinking it was blood; her rage left her and "her heart was filled with joy".

This myth demonstrates that the power of Sekhmet has the potential to become senselessly over-destructive, raging on heedless of the consequences. A necessary discipline is to keep in touch with the higher wisdom of far-seeing Ra and to know how and when to transmute the passion of rage into compassion and constructive action. A shared bottle of wine can re-establish a sense of common humanity.

The lioness is fiercely protective of her young, implacable and fearless in her attack on anything that threatens them. She is a skilled and ruthless hunter, often forming co-operative groups with other lionesses. She can be amazingly tender and nurturing to her cubs, yet her treatment of them is robust, tolerating no insubordination while encouraging energetic and challenging play.

All these qualities are found in Sekhmet. She is a symbol of proud, queenly power and confidence, of high self-esteem and of the mobilisation of the fiery will to make room for improvements by destroying the out-moded and restrictive. She can help us to rid ourselves of that aspect of human nature that tends to become a slave to habit, petty obligations and inertia. She gives us the energy to change, to achieve our goals, to bring our creative inspiration to fruition. She gives us the courage and that dash of ruthlessness that is necessary to break old patterns, a process that may make others uncomfortable, even angry. She empowers us in the dark days of winter and in the dark nights of the soul when self-doubt and depression stifle our creativity and make us feel disappointed in ourselves. Her fiery breath energises us, rouses us from lethargy and brings a new sense of decisiveness and assertiveness. Her roar reminds us that everyone has the right to make their voice heard and to be listened to with respect.

When we rebel against what restricts us, whether it is our lack of confidence and faith in our abilities, or habitual patterns that have built up in our lives, we may unleash strong feeling of anger against all those who seem to have put us in this position. Anger can be a very liberating force, giving us the power to assert ourselves, and energising us to make the necessary changes. But our anger needs to be kept in proportion by the higher wisdom of Ra, which shows us that unbridled rage can be both dangerous and *ridiculous*. Then is the anger turned into assertiveness and laughter, and our "hearts are filled with joy".

The lioness is queen of beasts: she does not need to rage, for few can threaten her. She knows how to relax, to let go and be sensuous, enjoying food and drink, play, companionship, a rest in the sun. But in a moment she can become fully alert, her senses finely tuned to her environment. The strength and power of Sekhmet allows us to have the confidence to be fully in the present time, neither regretting what is past nor worrying about the future, completely ready at all times to deal with zest with whatever life may bring.

Evoke her power within you when you feel down and powerless, trapped by the circumstances of your life. Evoke her when you desire to make changes in your life but seem to lack the will or courage to implement them. Evoke her when you need energy and confidence to cope with particular people or situations. Let her leonine power arise within you and you will find that self doubt and the confusion it brings replaced by a new clarity of vision and certitude.

# Sekhmet

Incense: Frankincense, Dragon's Blood, Rosemary

Hail, Sekhmet, Lion Queen, whose essence is Fire, tempestuous forever. Thou art throned in the desert in the heat of noon, crowned with the Uraeus of divine power and the Sun's disk. In thy right hand is the Ankh of eternal life, and thy left holds the papyrus sceptre. Thy voice is the roar of passionate will that none may gainsay.

Prowl thou the desert way of our being, O Lady of Flame; Send the reverberations of thy roar into the soul's deep canyons, shattering the silence, and awakening us to new vision and resolve. Thy breath is the hot flame that burns away the dry brushwood of our lives, freeing us for new ventures.

Wherever men and women walk tall and gaze meets
  gaze in fearless pride,

Wherever skill and strength unite with inspiration,

Wherever Will is ignited and noble aspiration blazes
  into action,

The heat of thy Fire inflames our blood.


By the blazing Sun at noon,

By the empowerment of Will Triumphant,

By heat and flame and spitting serpent,


I call upon thee to Be with Us

                    in Body and in Spirit.


*Jean M. William*

# The Morrigan

*W*hoever would want to invoke the Morrigan, the formidable Battle Goddess of the Irish Celts? Her name aptly means "Phantom Queen" and she was said to appear as a terrifying black crow over the battle field, screaming and taunting the warriors. She was also seen mounted on a black horse, riding the storm clouds over the battle field, bearing on her arm the great shield of protection and in her right hand the fearsome spear of her indomitable will. She was also called "The Washer at the Ford", and might be seen washing the clothes of those about to die in battle; for anyone who saw her doing this, it was a presentiment of their death.

The Morrigan was the protector of the land and the home. When outsiders attacked, whether for pillage and booty or conquest, the Morrigan could be called upon to strengthen and inspire the defenders, filling them with courage, and striking terror into the hearts of the invaders. She gives her followers that psychological edge that brings victory, even against great odds.

It is this that gives a clue to her modern relevance. She is the goddess of desperate causes. When you feel that your rights are denied, your space invaded, your future threatened or your freedom curtailed, then may you call on the Morrigan. It is her spirit that enables an isolated individual to take a stand against bullies or to blow the whistle on incompetent or dishonest bosses. She gives people the power and the courage to make their voices heard and to draw others of like mind to their cause. She could be seen as the goddess of the Greenham Common women who felt passionately that this planet and their children's future were threatened by the cold war and the proliferation of nuclear weapons; also as the goddess of the suffragettes, who fought for the rights of women to vote, and of people persecuted for challenging the abuse of power by those in authority. She is the goddess to call on when the media invade the privacy and defame the way of life of ordinary people with few financial resources, twisting the truth to make a titillating story.

There are dangers in calling on such a powerful and confrontational goddess. The sense of a shared cause and the joy of battle can be very seductive so that when the immediate goal has been achieved, there may be a reluctance to step back and make peace, to accept others' points of view and perhaps to agree some compromises for the sake of amity and the common good. It is all too easy at this point to nurse a sense of grievance and to seek total victory rather than being prepared to find a practical solution. Although most of us count ourselves as civilised, using the weapons of words, the legal system and peaceful demonstration rather than sword or spear (or bomb), the world is full of the pain of extremist terrorism. And most terrorism is fuelled by a sense of injustice that is based on at least a small kernel of truth, even though the event that gave rise to it may have happened in the distant past.

When the exhilaration of battle and the scent of victory seem to lure us on to prolong the conflict, then it is well to remember that the Morrigan is the defender of the home and the land. She is not the goddess of revenge, nor the goddess of conquest. Not knowing when to stop may endanger the very cause we were defending and lose the gains that have been made. Then we may see the Morrigan washing *our* clothes at the ford!

The Morrigan gives us the courage to take on just causes and to stand up for ourselves, to speak out, but her earthy wisdom also aids us in assessing the strength of the forces we are up against and in working out the best strategies. To aim for small achievable goals in the short term may serve the cause better than an ambitious long-term confrontation. The hotheads may see this as a sell-out, but the Morrigan's passion ensures that we do not lose sight of the long-term goals. She empowers us to continue to pursue the causes of freedom and justice, even from generation to generation. She can be seen as the evolutionary force behind the long-term struggles against sexism, racism, religious bigotry and the worst aspects of capitalism.

When we evoke her qualities within us, we find the courage to speak and to act. But, equally important, we also develop the wisdom to identify the "enemy" correctly and to define immediate and long-term goals. We can then choose appropriate words and actions to pursue our just cause.

# The Morrigan

Incense: Pine resin, Yew leaves, Myrrh

O Thou, Morrigan, Warrior Queen of Battles! Raven-haired and raven-winged, thou ridest the storm. On thine arm is the mighty shield of protection and thou wieldest the spear of thy formidable Will. Thy voice is the scream of the wind and the shriek of the hawk as it stoops to its kill. None may close their ears to thy voice!

Fly thou into the heart of the storm, Mistress of terror and exultation. Phantom Queen, Black Crow of Night, awaken us to the joy of battle. Courage blazes from the flashing point of thy spear, calling us to sacrifice – even unto death. Yet wilt thou continue to sustain the truth of our cause, throughout the long night of battle, until the Sun shall rise victorious and a new day dawn, and the world be remade in justice, peace and freedom.

Wherever women rage against patriarchy,

Wherever rebellion gathers against unjust laws and the tyranny of government,

Wherever citizens pit their puny strength against the vested interest of powerful organisations,

Wherever bigotry and intolerance threaten our freedoms,

There is the scream of thy battle cry heard!

By the Courage that is born of desperation,

By the Passion that gives a voice to Reason,

By the Wisdom of the just cause,

By shield and spear and black raven's feather,

I call upon thee to Be with Us
                              in Body and in Spirit.

*Jean M.Williams*

# Bibliography

*W*e have not burdened the text of the essays with references. But we gratefully acknowledge our debt to the following main sources of information and ideas.

General:
*Larousse Encyclopedia of Mythology*; Paul Hamlyn, 1964

On the Graeco-Roman pantheon:
*The Greek Myths;* Graves, Robert; Penguin Books, 1960
*Hermes the Thief*; Brown, Norman O.; Vintage Books, 1969
*The Mythic Tarot*; Sharman-Burke, Juliet, and Greene, Liz; Rider, 1986

On the Egyptian Pantheon:
*Bast and Sekhmet*; Constantine, Storm and Coquio, Eloise; Robert Hale, 1999
*The Gods of the Egyptians* Vols.1 and 2; Wallis Budge, E.A.; Dover Publications, 1969